prophecies

prophecies

4,000 years of prophets,
visionaries and predictions

Tony Allan

**BARNES
&NOBLE**

——————
NEW YORK

prophecies

Tony Allan

This edition published by Barnes & Noble, Inc., by arrangement with Duncan Baird Publishers

2006 Barnes & Noble Books

M 10 9 8 7 6 5 4 3 2 1

ISBN-10: 0-7607-8176-1
ISBN-13: 978-0-7607-8176-0

Design: Richard Wise and Jeremy Pearce at 2wo Design
Project Editor: Joanne Clay
Picture Researcher: Julia Ruxton
Managing Editor: Christopher Westhorp
Managing Designer: Manisha Patel

Library of Congress Cataloguing-in-Publication Data is available

Typeset in Democratica and Filosofia
Colour reproduction by Scanhouse, Malaysia
Printed in Singapore by Imago

NOTES
The abbreviations CE and BCE are used throughout this book:
BCE Before the Common Era (the equivalent of BC)
CE Common Era (the equivalent of AD)

FRONTISPIECE: Portrait of a seer or somnambulist by the French artist Gustave Courbet (1819–1877).
RIGHT: Illustration from the frontispiece of a 16th-century edition of A Little Book of Love *by the Elizabethan occultist John Dee (see pages 99–101).*

contents

introduction

In the beginning, prophecy meant the word of God. The biblical prophets were so called not because they foretold what was to come, but because they bore a divine message. In Islamic tradition, too, Muhammad was the Prophet because he spoke for Allah, not because he prognosticated on forthcoming events. The same point held true even in cultures that recognized many gods; there too, shamans credited with a range of prophetic powers owed their authority to their claim to speak with the voice of the spirits.

From early on, though, the idea of the future insinuated itself into the prophets' armoury, and in time it became its most important component, making the very word "prophetic" synonymous with "prescient" or "predictive". Reflection suggests that the reason for the switch was connected with the nature of prophetic authority itself. The seers' prestige rested on their ability to tap otherwise inaccessible sources of knowledge. The information that was consistently most in demand from their audience concerned the likely prospects for the community to which they reported. Anyone who could reliably say what was going to happen before it occurred was in a uniquely privileged position to win the public's ear.

It is prophecy's grasp of the future that has ensured its relevance up to the present day. In one sense we are all prophets, in that we constantly have to make predictions, conscious or otherwise, about what the coming days, months and years might hold in store. Every business-man making a strategic decision, every householder mulling an investment or selecting a holiday, every gambler putting money on a horse – all must sometimes have had the sinking feeling that their lives are in the grip of some fearful, dumb beast called the Future that can undo the best-laid plans with a single twist of fate. Knowing what this behemoth holds in store is the key to success or failure in all our longterm projects. No other form of knowledge is as crucial or as difficult to attain.

This book seeks to explore prophecy in all its major forms. The first chapter specifically examines those prophets who have claimed to speak as mouthpieces for the gods. It shows how, by classical times, some of these divine spokespersons were already putting their knowledge to use to forecast future developments. The oracle at Delphi was only the best known of a host of similar Greek and Roman shrines where individuals could learn what their personal destiny was likely to be.

However, an unexpected subtext in this chapter is the strand in the prophetic tradition that looks not to the future so much as back to the past. This tendency often finds expression in apocalyptic predictions of disasters to come. Such pessimism is typically the province of peoples threatened by abrupt culture change, for whom the golden age has already been and gone. In such circumstances the

A coloured woodcut from L'Atmosphère: Météorologie Populaire *(1888), by the French astronomer and science writer Camille Flammarion, shows a begowned seeker of esoteric knowledge crawling on his knees through the firmament of the fixed stars, and thus "breaking through" the medieval conception of the universe.*

best their prophets can offer is often the prospect of a future age when the old ways will be restored.

Subsequent chapters concentrate on other routes to knowledge of the future (although it is important to remember that at least some of these were claimed to have had the sanction of divine authority). They include dreams and premonitions – which cultures around the world have traditionally regarded as offering occasional pinpoints of illumination – and divination, which seeks to trap the gift of prediction within the confines of a structured system. A survey of seers and clairvoyants concentrates on individuals who, although they may have claimed to speak in God's name, operated outside the established Church, or, like Nostradamus, concerned themselves primarily with secular matters.

The final chapter shifts the focus again to more modern forms of prophecy that attempt to work out forthcoming developments by the exercise of human reason alone. The logical culmination of this tendency is the present vogue for scientific forecasting, which now affects almost every aspect of life in Western societies. Yet rational prediction has limitations of its own – while excellent at projecting existing trends, it has so far proved largely ineffective at giving advance warning of discontinuities. Despite the best efforts of planners and think tanks, the unexpected continues to happen.

There have been relatively few general overviews of prophecy and prediction of the type attempted here. Geoffrey Ashe's excellent *Book of Prophecy* is one notable recent exception. In some ways the paucity is surprising, given the importance of the subject, but in part the gap is filled by the many almanacs and astrological works that pretend to offer some knowledge of the future. This book makes no such claims, although it does include some so-far unfulfilled predictions on the part of prophets who did.

What *Prophecies* does aim to show is that there are patterns in the phenomenon of prophecy itself – an upwelling of interest in times of crisis, a lingering fascination in eras of great change. Prophecy, it suggests,

Death, the thirteenth card in the tarot sequence known as the Major Arcana. Tarot cards are one of the most popular divinatory accessories in the Western world today.

is a psychological necessity for humankind. People simply cannot contemplate the terrible uncertainties of the future without it, and in the last resort will regularly turn to false prophets rather than have no prophets at all. If the book has a conscious goal other than to interest and entertain, it is to make past experience serve as a guide to the good prophets – and, for the rest, to instil a degree of open-minded scepticism in the reader about the large claims that prophets have always promised to fulfill.

mouthpieces of the gods

If prophecy is inspired utterance, its roots lie in trance. Modern psychiatry tends to dismiss trance as mere self-hypnosis, but in the past the trance state was regarded with awe as an ecstatic condition permitting direct communion with the gods. In its grip, the individual literally lost him- or herself and became a mouthpiece for a god or spirit.

The message the prophet bore could take various forms. The classical world inherited, possibly from Asia, a tradition of possessed women; channelled through interpreters, the women's incoherent ravings were the foundations on which the great oracles of Greece and Rome were built. However, in theocratically-inclined Israel prophecy took on a very different role, as a tool of moral correction. A chain of individuals claiming to be inspired by the holy Yahweh came forward to denounce the sins of a wayward people and to foretell disaster if the nation failed to change its ways.

Finally, there was a long and cosmopolitan line of exceptional men and women, each convinced of their own divinely-inspired mission. From Joan of Arc in medieval France to Hong Xiuquang, the Taiping leader in nineteenth-century China, these mavericks had little in common but their own self-belief — but that in itself could sometimes be powerful enough to change the world.

the roots of prophecy

This rattle with a carved hawk face belonged to a shaman of the Tsimshian people of British Columbia. Shamans used such instruments to accompany their ritual chanting and call up supernatural power from other unseen worlds.

The roots of prophecy – if indeed it began as inspired utterance – must lie in shamanism, the animistic belief in a world populated by spirits that was the earliest and most enduring religion. The origins of shamanism lie deep in humankind's hunter-gatherer past, and predate the written word by several millennia. Although the term "shaman", meaning a priest of shamanism, comes from Siberia, where the phenomenon was widespread until recent times, shamans and their rites have been found in different forms on every continent. Shamanism continues to be practised in many parts of the world to this day.

Although prophecy in its wider sense was part of the shaman's art, foretelling future events played only a small role in what he – or, more rarely, she – set out to achieve. What all shamans claimed to have was access to information not available to the mass of humankind. This knowledge came from the spirits that the shamans encountered on their voyages, for they were mental travellers whose souls left their bodies. The journeys the shamans made sometimes took them to the realms of gods, or to distant parts of the real world. They brought back intelligence that could be put to use for the good of the village or the tribe.

The vehicle the shaman used for these journeys was the trance state, and shamans in different parts of the world used various means to attain it. Music and dance were frequent aids, as were some hallucinogenic

Japan's prophetess queen

Early legends from Japan, on the cusp between myth and history, tell of a queen named Himiko or Pimiko. She was the first known Japanese ruler and the legendary founder of the great Shinto shrine at Ise. Himiko seems to have had special links to the sun goddess Amaterasu: the written characters that represent the queen's name mean "sun child", and stories tell that she had custody of Amaterasu's sacred mirror. Himiko was unmarried, and lived in a heavily guarded palace where she communed with her divine ancestors, passing on through a male intermediary the messages that she received from the spirits. Chinese records confirm that there was indeed a queen of that name in the first century BCE, and state that on her death she was laid to rest in a huge burial mound, and followed to the grave by more than 100 attendants.

Ancient Native American rock art at the "Shaman's Gallery" site in the Grand Canyon area of the upper Colorado Plateau. There are glimpses of similar practices in early cave art in Europe and in prehistoric Aboriginal rock paintings in Australia, suggesting the shamanistic tradition is an ancient one worldwide.

substances. In Mexico, women healers took psilocybe mushrooms; the Yanomami of the Amazon rain forest employed several powders, including one made from the dried inner bark of the virola tree.

The shamans' trance-journeys
Different cultures interpreted the shamanistic soul-flight in terms of their own traditions. Among the best-known examples are the Inuit stories of the Sea Mother, Sedna. Inuit hunters depended on a regular supply of game to see them through the long Arctic winter. Whenever game was in short supply, it was assumed that Sedna was angry, offended by some thoughtless contravention of taboo, and was taking her revenge by hoarding the animals she controlled. In such circumstances a shaman would make

the long and dangerous spiritual voyage to Sedna's sea-bed home. While villagers sang and chanted to help him on his way, the visionary would enter an extended trance, setting off on a quest in which he could expect to encounter fearsome obstacles. When he arrived, he had to appease the Sea Mother and persuade her to release the seals, walruses and other creatures that the villagers needed. If he was successful, the community could expect plentiful hunting in the months to come, and the shaman would be duly honoured for the vital task he had performed.

Besides providing game in times of need, shamans around the world had many other functions. Healing was a principal one, for they were the doctors of early societies, undertaking trance-journeys to learn the causes and cures of illnesses and

afflictions. In addition, the shamans brought news of the fate of missing persons, sought rain in times of drought and helped secure victory for their own side's warriors in times of war. Shamans could also wander in time, journeying forward to learn the likely outcome of a battle or the course of a disease.

Memories of the shamans' trance-journeys linger in all the early descriptions of inspired utterance. The common thread linking Hebrew prophets (see pages 12–15) to the Pythia at Delphi (see pages 24–7) and the oracles of Bronze Age Africa (see pages 92–3) or ancient Peru (see pages 94–7) lies in this shared tradition: one of exceptional individuals able temporarily to attain ecstatic, visionary states in which the hidden became visible and the unknown was revealed.

The old testament prophets

Over the centuries, Western views of prophecy and prophets have been shaped more by the Bible than by any other source. From the Old Testament comes the image of the *illuminatus* inspired by Yahweh to call down woe on his erring people and to predict disaster for all who do not follow his ways. Yet the status of prophets in ancient Israel and Judah was, in fact, more complex than that picture would suggest.

Nabis and kings
The earliest prophets mentioned in the Old Testament in many ways still recalled the old, shamanist tradition. The prophets, or *nabi*s, as they were known (*nabi* means someone with a vocation), were a class of inspired individuals who existed alongside and apart from the Jewish priesthood. The *nabi*s wore skin garments, played musical instruments and invoked the divine spirit. When it passed into them, they prophesied and had visions; sometimes they stripped naked in their ecstasy.

There is a vivid description of such people in 1 Samuel 10, when the prophet Samuel tells Saul: "As you come to the city, you will meet a band of prophets coming down from the high place with the harp, tambourine, flute and lyre before them, prophesying. Then the Spirit of the Lord will come mightily upon you, and you shall prophesy with them and be turned into another man". Saul duly did so, to the amazement of onlookers, who asked, "Is Saul also among the prophets?"

While it was obviously thought surprising for a future king of Israel to keep such company, what is interesting about this story is that the encounter could have happened at all. The scene shows that the prophets were still seen as men of God and were not necessarily in conflict with authority. In fact, their relationship with the secular power could even be

Old Testament prophets Hosea and Amos with the Archangel Uriel, depicted in a fresco in Avignon's medieval Palace of the Popes.

too cosy, as a subsequent story suggests. This tale, from 1 Kings 22, recounts how King Ahab consulted no fewer than 400 prophets before undertaking a military adventure, and was assured of success by every one. Only when an independent voice was consulted was there any dissent – the notoriously stubborn Micaiah insisted that God had given them all lying tongues to deceive Ahab. Events proved him correct.

> "And the spirit of god came upon [saul] also; and as he went he prophesied, until he came to naioth in ramah. And he too stripped off his clothes, and he too prophesied before samuel, and lay naked all that day and all that night."
>
> (1 SAMUEL 19. 23–24, DESCRIBING KING SAUL'S TIME WITH THE ECSTATIC PROPHETS)

Prophets of punishment

From the eighth century BCE on a new kind of prophet appeared in Israel. Amos was the first of the literary prophets, who raised their voices less in ecstatic utterance than in reasoned denunciation of luxury, immorality and, above all, apostasy. In many ways the newcomers were moralists before they were seers, dedicated to chastizing the sins of the people and to warning of disasters to come if the Israelites failed to mend their ways. However, these prophets were believed to be in direct communion with the Lord, and it was thought that they could sometimes use his foreknowledge to predict events. So Jeremiah could forecast both the Babylonian domination and the devastation of Babylon itself that would ultimately follow it: "This whole land [of Judah] shall become a ruin … , and these nations shall serve the king of Babylon for 70 years. Then … I will punish the king of Babylon and that nation, the land of the Chaldeans, for their iniquity, says the Lord, making the land an everlasting waste" (Jeremiah 25. 11–12).

The period between the fall of Jerusalem to the Babylonians in 597BCE and the capture of Babylon by the Persians in 538BCE was actually closer to 60 than to 70 years, but the gist of Jeremiah's words still proved remarkably accurate. As for the devastation of Babylon, the few remaining mounds of rubble standing south of modern-day Baghdad are proof enough of the truth of the prophet's vision.

A forbidden tradition

The Old Testament makes it clear that other divinatory traditions were known in ancient Israel, but were strictly proscribed. With practitioners of Chaldean astrology very much in mind, Deuteronomy 18 laid down that: "There shall not be found among you … anyone who practises divination, a soothsayer or an augur … for whoever does those things is an abomination to the Lord". Yet the story of the Witch of Endor in 1 Samuel 28 shows that such practices continued, despite the strictures of the law. It relates how King Saul, during his war against the Philistines, found that the accepted ways of ascertaining the Lord's will had all failed him; he had received no enlightenment from dreams, prophets or the Urim (sacred objects used to divine the future by lot). So the king disguised himself and went to consult the witch, who duly raised the spirit of the deceased prophet Samuel from the grave to advise Saul. Although the biblical account unambiguously condemns necromancy – the practice of consulting the dead – as illegal and the act of a desperate man, it also indicates that it worked.

The coming of the messiah

The best known of all biblical prophecies concerns the coming of the Messiah. The word itself, which means "anointed one" in Hebrew, denotes someone with a special mission from the Lord. In the Old Testament the term is, in fact, applied to various patriarchs and prophets, and even to the Persian king Cyrus, who delivered the Jews from their Babylonian captivity.

As time passed and the political situation in Israel worsened, the term came to have a more specific application. The Messiah was to be a future king, born of the line of David, sent by God to deliver Israel from bondage and to usher in a new golden age.

In the Old Testament the Messiah is not generally associated with the Last Days – the time of trial leading up to the world's end. However, in the last two centuries BCE, the belief took on a distinctly eschatological tinge. (Derived from the Greek *eskhatos*, meaning "last", the word eschatological signifies beliefs concerning the final times.) The impetus for this development seems to have come from the traumatic shock suffered by devout Jews during the reign of Antiochus IV Epiphanes. In the interests of encouraging Hellenization, Antiochus, a ruler of the Greek Seleucid dynasty, banned all Jewish religious observances, thereby inspiring the Maccabean revolt in the middle of the second century BCE. Faced with the suppression of all that they believed in, the faithful responded with retributive dreams of a warrior-saviour, who would not only trample down their enemies, but also set in motion the process by which the righteous would ultimately inherit the Earth.

The fullest expression of the new vision came in the book of Daniel, thought to have been written at the time of the revolt. In a dream, the prophet saw four symbolic beasts representing the foreign powers that had ruled Israel, the Babylonians and Persians among them. In Daniel's vision the fourth such power, the Seleucid dynasty, was swept away by a divine emissary, the Son of Man, who came as the Lord's representative to establish an earthly kingdom covering all peoples and all lands. However, although the Maccabees did succeed in restoring religious freedom for the Jews and, eventually, in establishing a native dynasty on the throne, no Son of Man appeared. The great messianic dream had to be postponed for later generations.

The birth of the promised one

Expectations of divine intervention rose again after the Roman annexation of Palestine in 63BCE. The Jews once more chafed under foreign overlords; the divine assurance that they were chosen over other peoples again seemed hard to believe. It was into an atmosphere of

> "And behold, with the clouds of heaven there came one like a son of man, and he came to the Ancient of Days and was presented before him. And to him was given dominion and glory and kingdom, that all peoples, nations, and languages should serve him; his dominion is an everlasting dominion, which shall not pass away."
>
> (DANIEL'S PROPHECY OF THE COMING MESSIAH, DANIEL 7. 13–14)

The Resurrection of Christ – *one of three panels from the Isenheim Altarpiece – was painted ca.1512–1516 by Matthias Grünewald. Christ the Messiah is shown rising into the sky with his hands raised in blessing against the background of a halo-like sun.*

suppressed nationalist longing that Jesus was born. Early on in his ministry his followers, the apostles, decided that Jesus might indeed be the promised Messiah, and bestowed on him the title of Christos or Christ, the Greek equivalent of the Hebrew term. Theologians still argue over the extent to which Jesus himself encouraged such speculation, although Matthew 16 seems unambiguous on the point. There, Jesus specifically identifies himself as the Son of Man mentioned in Daniel's prophecy. More remarkably still, he tells the apostles that "there are some standing here who will not taste death before they see the Son of Man coming into his kingdom".

Jesus's words appeared to promise that the "end time" was at hand, and the first Christians duly interpreted the utterance in that light. His prophecy was similarly viewed by his enemies – the main charge brought against Jesus after his arrest by the Jewish high priest Caiaphas was that he claimed to be the Christ or Messiah. Pontius Pilate, the Roman governor of Judea who sentenced Jesus to death, asked the accused whether he was indeed the promised King of the Jews.

At the time of Jesus's death in ca. 30CE, and for many years afterward, some believers continued to expect an imminent Second Coming that would sweep away all oppression and injustice. Only gradually, when this failed to materialize, did Christians learn to take Jesus's words in a spiritual sense, seeing the spread of the Church as fulfilling the first part of his mission, while his return in glory was put off to an unspecified future time.

Meanwhile the Jews, who had never accepted the Christians' claims, continued to await a messiah of their own. Expectations of his arrival helped fuel the disastrous revolt of 66–70CE, which led to the destruction of the Temple in Jerusalem. Such expectations were also instrumental in stirring up the last revolt against Roman rule – that of Simeon Bar Kokhba in 132–135CE. Bar Kokhba himself, a tough guerrilla commander, was hailed at the time as the promised Messiah. In fact, the rebellion was put down brutally, Bar Kokhba was killed, and repressive Roman counter-measures hastened the Jewish diaspora from Palestine. The messianic dream was not lost, but for many centuries it was exiled overseas.

The Reign of the Antichrist

A second prophecy inextricably linked with that of the Messiah (see pages 14–15) concerned his antithesis and arch-foe, the Antichrist. Although it obviously found its full expression in the Christian era, this prediction also had roots in the Old Testament. There are even clear indications of who the original Antichrist – although anti-Messiah would, in the context, be a more appropriate term – might have been: Antiochus IV Epiphanes, the same ruler whose impious actions first stimulated Jewish hopes of a messiah.

For, in the same vision in which Daniel foresaw the coming of the Son of Man, he also described the evil one the Messiah would come to replace. The details were precise. Daniel saw four beasts, representing the foreign powers that had ruled Israel, and he linked the anti-Messiah to the fourth of them, symbolizing the Seleucid Greeks who ruled Israel in the wake of Alexander the Great in the second century BCE. Daniel claimed that 10 kings would precede the anti-Messiah – and Antiochus was indeed the 11th king of the Seleucid dynasty. The anti-Messiah would in turn defeat three kings, just as Antiochus had conquered two Egyptian pharaohs and a ruler of Cyprus. Then again, the evil one would speak blasphemously and "wear out the saints of the Most High"; he would "think to change the times and the law", as Antiochus did in forbidding the Jews from practising the hallowed rites that the Mosaic law commanded. But a day would come, predicted Daniel, when the anti-Messiah's dominion would be taken away and the "greatness of the kingdoms under the whole Heaven" would be given to the saints – a promise partly fulfilled in the success of the Maccabean revolt, which liberated

The defeat of the Antichrist is portrayed in a panel from La Leyenda de San Miguel (The Legend of Saint Michael) *painted ca. 1450 by the Spanish artist known as the Master of Arguis.*

Eastern influences?

Some people have seen Persian influences in the prophecy of the Antichrist. Zoroastrian legend tells of a time of trial preceding the last age in which Ahriman, the Evil One, will unleash his forces, and terrible devastation will result. But the great warrior Keresaspa will be despatched from Heaven to slay Ahriman's chief weapon, the foul dragon Azhi Dahaka, and a promised era of peace and eternal harmony will ensue.

Jerusalem and restored the old rites, even if it did not pass universal dominion to the Jews.

Christ's Second Coming

In seeing Jesus as the final fulfilment of the Son of Man prophecy, the early Christians also inherited the Antichrist elements attached to it. In a letter preserved in the New Testament, the apostle John warned followers of the early Church that "many antichrists" had already come, showing that the last hour was at hand. He went on to define the Antichrist as "one who denies the Father and the Son". Without mentioning the word, St Paul in his second letter to the Thessalonians also alluded to an Antichrist figure, although he seemed to have had a much more precise enemy in mind. Calling him the "lawless one", a supposed worker of wonders who would first have to be exposed before the day of the Lord could dawn, Paul specifically identified him as one "who takes his seat in the temple of God, proclaiming himself to be God". Almost certainly Paul had in mind the Roman emperors, who were then proclaiming their own divinity.

Gradually, in the early Middle Ages, the traditions of the impious ruler and the deceitful wonder-worker were combined. Two influential prophetic books – so-called Sibylline texts, named after the oracular books that Rome's leaders often consulted (see page 29) – painted a clear picture of the events leading up to Christ's Second Coming. They introduced the figure of a great Christian ruler, the Emperor of the Last Days, who would defeat Christ's enemies. The most terrible of these foes would be Gog of the land of Magog (see page 21), a mighty ruler from the north who would only be defeated after a titanic struggle. In the wake of his triumph the Christian emperor would travel to Jerusalem to lay down his crown. Yet before Christ's reappearance, there would be a brief but terrible interlude in which the Antichrist would seize power, deceiving many by supposed miracles and horribly persecuting the faithful who were not taken in by his trickery. The Antichrist's reign would be a final time of trial for the just, but it would not last for long. God would strike down the usurper, and Christ would appear in glory to inaugurate his reign on Earth, which would last for a thousand years until the Last Judgment.

Throughout the Middle Ages, millions of people across Europe waited for this pattern to unfold. Whenever a strong Christian ruler appeared, hopes rose that he might be the promised emperor. Each time a persecutor struck down the faithful, believers sought consolation in the belief that the Second Coming might be at hand. Even now, the prophecy is very much alive, and predictions of the Antichrist's birth continue to be made.

> "The coming of the lawless one by the activity of satan will be with all power and with pretended signs and wonders, and with all wicked deception for those who are to perish, because they refused to love the truth and so be saved."
>
> (PAUL'S SECOND LETTER TO THE THESSALONIANS 2. 9–10 ON THE COMING OF THE ANTICHRIST)

The Apocalypse of st John

No-one would dispute that, in the Christian world at least, the most influential prophetic book in the Bible is the last: the Revelation to John, or book of Revelation as it was long known. It is a relatively short text of just 23 chapters, written in a visionary style of great poetic force. Some of its images – the Four Horsemen of the Apocalypse, the Number of the Beast, the New Jerusalem – have entered the public imagination and are familiar to people who have never read the book itself. In addition, the Revelation is a highly complex work that has lent itself to more divergent interpretations than almost any other text in world literature.

The author gives his name as "John", and it was long believed that he was the same John who wrote the fourth gospel. The attribution has been questioned on grounds of style, but it is supported by at least one reliable early witness – Irenaeus. A native of Asia Minor in the early second century CE and future bishop of Lyons, Irenaeus had known people in John's circle in his youth. Irenaeus also provided a date for the composition of the Revelation: late in the reign of the Roman emperor Domitian, near the end of the first century CE.

Hope born out of trauma

The date is significant. The Revelation text is late by biblical standards, and a great deal had happened since the time of Christ's own ministry in the reigns of the first two Roman emperors, Augustus and Tiberius. Since Jesus's crucifixion, three events of particularly traumatic significance had struck the early Christian Church.

The first occurred in the reign of Nero, emperor from 54 to 68CE and an unstable, possibly mad, ruler. In the year 64CE a terrible fire had destroyed much of the city of Rome, and public opinion blamed the emperor personally for the disaster. Not only were there stories of Nero, who had some talent as a musician, "fiddling while Rome burned", but rumour also suggested that the emperor had had the fire started for the pleasure of watching the flames. Word of these stories reached Nero himself, and he determined to find a scapegoat onto which he could transfer the blame. The Christians – a small but growing community whose beliefs were considered outlandish and who had incurred imperial displeasure by refusing to worship the emperor as a god – came quickly to mind. An unknown number of Christians were rounded up. Accused of arson, they were condemned to horrific deaths: some were set on fire as human torches, others

St John the Evangelist is portrayed receiving divine inspiration to write the Apocalypse in an engraving by Albrecht Dürer dated 1496.

The book of Revelation purports to be a simple record of what its author saw, under angelic guidance, on the tiny Greek island of Patmos in the Dodecanese group, 37 miles (60 km) off the coast of Asia Minor. This depiction of St John writing the Revelation on Patmos is by Berto di Giovanni (who died before 1629).

were crucified, some were covered in animal skins and fed to wild beasts in the Colosseum.

The second trauma that left its imprint on the Revelation was the defeat of the Jewish revolt and the fall of Jerusalem to the Romans in 70CE. The rebellion, inspired by zealots expecting the coming of their own messiah, was put down with terrible brutality. In its wake the Temple was destroyed and the priesthood abolished, while the taxes that had supported the Temple were diverted to the imperial treasury at Rome.

Like most early Christians, the author of the Revelation was still very much a Jew. The disasters that had befallen the Jewish people were recent events when

> " ... and great hailstones, heavy as a hundredweight, dropped on men from heaven, till men cursed god for the plague of the hail ... ."
>
> (DESCRIPTION IN THE BOOK OF REVELATION OF THE DAY OF WRATH, WHEN GOD'S ANGER WILL SMITE THE WORLD)

The Dragon Waging War and the Beast of the Sea, *from the 13th-century French-school Apocalypse Miniatures. Writing the Apocalypse, St John drew on the prophet Daniel's vision of a 10-horned beast rising from the sea. For Daniel, this figure had represented the Greek Seleucid dynasty, which was oppressing the Jews in his day (see page 16). For John, the persecuting empire was Domitian's Rome, and the target was the worldwide Christian community.*

he was writing, still raw in popular memory. When the audience for the Revelation heard prophecies of the New Jerusalem, the largely-destroyed Jerusalem of old would have loomed large in their minds.

Worse still, the very people who had led the oppression of the Jews had gone on to rule the empire of which not just Judea but most of the known world was now a part. Vespasian, the commander originally sent to suppress the revolt, had been proclaimed emperor at Rome even before the job was finished. The suppression was completed by Vespasian's son Titus, who in time succeeded his father on the imperial throne.

Then, in 81CE, Titus died and was succeeded by his younger brother Domitian, a cruel and tyrannical emperor who insisted on being addressed as "Lord and God". Under his rule, the first systematic persecution of the Christians began – the third traumatic event providing the backdrop for John's Apocalypse. Under Domitian, executions for treason were rife, spies were everywhere and Christianity was proscribed. The position of the believers to whom John addressed his

message was that of a small but passionately committed dissident minority in a totalitarian state. Much of the apparent obscurity of John's words can only be understood against this backdrop. His writings were unauthorized and illegal, and were passed around clandestinely. Many of the ideas they sought to convey could only be hinted at, not stated openly.

The end of time

What John's vision had to communicate was nothing less than an overview of the future of the world. He expressed it in terms that leaned heavily on Old Testament prophetic tradition. He was inspired, for example, by Ezekiel's vision of a climactic, "end-time" battle between Israel and the people of Gog and Magog (see box, opposite).

In addition to the 10-horned beast representing Rome (see image, above), John also introduced a two-horned beast that "makes the earth and its inhabitants worship the first beast". This was probably a symbol for the imperial cult that required citizens of the empire to worship the emperor as a god. It is in the context of this second creature that John spoke of the "number of the beast", using it to identify the specific target he had in mind. "This calls for wisdom," he wrote. "Let him who has understanding reckon the number of the beast, for it is a human number, and its number is 666." John was clearly using a numerical code. In his day, Arabic numerals were still to come, and letters were used to represent figures – for example, the Roman "C" stood for "100". Many ingenious attempts have been made to work out the identity of the beast by adding up various Latin and Greek combinations, but all were almost certainly misguided. With security in mind, John had reverted to his native Hebrew, in which the formula *Neron Kaisar* – the normal Greek form for writing "Emperor Nero" at the time – added up exactly to the required number.

Up to this point there was nothing prophetic in John's vision of the Roman beast swallowing up the faithful; he was merely describing the world as he saw it. However, in the latter stages of the Revelation he moved well beyond the present to distant future times. John's vision was nothing if not specific. He saw a great conflict between the beasts' forces and those of a heavenly warrior on a white horse backed by 144,000 of the faithful – images of

> "And in the spirit he carried me away to a great, high mountain, and showed me the holy city Jerusalem coming down out of heaven from god, having the glory of god, its radiance like a most rare jewel, like a jasper, clear as crystal."

(JOHN'S VISION OF THE DESCENT OF THE NEW JERUSALEM FROM THE BOOK OF REVELATION 21. 10–11)

Christ and the Christian Church. After terrible slaughter the righteous carry the day, and Christ and the risen martyrs then rule the world for a thousand years. At the end of that time, Satan, who has been consigned to the bottomless pit, is loosed again and raises a revolt, backed by the forces of Gog and Magog, who besiege Jerusalem. But flames come from Heaven to consume them, and Satan is hurled into a lake of fire. The Last Judgment follows, in which the righteous dead are saved and the rest are cast into the flames. Yet the vision goes even beyond that, to foresee the birth of a new Heaven and Earth, and the descent of the New Jerusalem (see box, above). There the resurrected faithful live for ever, illuminated by the divine radiance.

Dealing as it does with the end of time, much of the imagery of the Apocalypse lies in the realm of faith rather than of rational judgment. Yet in its treatment of the Roman empire's fate at least, John's vision proved largely accurate. The Church did, after all, outlive the empire, just as John foresaw, and with the barbarian invasions of the fifth century CE, the city of Rome itself was cast down as he had also predicted.

The gog-magog prophecy

One element of the Revelation doomsday scenario that has attracted particular attention is the assault on Jerusalem by the army of Gog and Magog, the defeat of which will signal the hour of the Last Judgment. The passage echoes a similar prophecy in the Old Testament book of Ezekiel, in which "Gog, of the land of Magog", identified as being in "the uttermost parts of the north", launches an assault on Israel at the head of a coalition of powers. There have been many attempts to identify Gog: in the 1950s there was a vogue for linking it with Stalin's USSR. Yet the expected Soviet invasion of Israel never happened, and with the break-up of the USSR such fears receded – rightly so, literal readers of the text would say, since according to John the attack will only follow after the thousand-year reign of the saints.

A Divine Madness

The spirit of prophecy permeated classical Greece and Rome. In real life few important decisions were taken without consulting diviners or oracles, and in myth too individuals with clairvoyant powers played a significant part. Almost invariably the myths portray these individuals as tragic figures, who were cursed, rather than blessed, with a terrible gift. For example, the Trojan princess Cassandra was given foresight by the god Apollo as a reward for agreeing to sleep with him, but she subsequently went back on her promise. To punish her, Apollo condemned her always to know what was going to happen but never to be believed. Similarly, the seer Tiresias only received his ability to foretell the future from Zeus as a compensation for being struck blind by Zeus's wife Hera. Tiresias had offended the goddess by insisting, when asked whether men or women most enjoyed the act of sex, that women's pleasure was nine times more intense.

Diviners and visionaries

There were, in fact, two distinct prophetic traditions that coexisted in classical times: Plato, in his dialogue the *Phaedo*, qualified them respectively as "sane" and "insane". The "sane" tradition involved divination following established rules of observation and interpretation; many different types were practised, including astrology, the casting of lots, and augury by studying the flight of birds or inspecting the livers of dead animals (see chapter 3). The "insane"

Prophets in Greek myth rarely came to a good end. Like Cassandra, Laocoön foresaw disaster for the city of Troy if the Greeks' wooden horse was taken within the walls. For his pains he was consumed by a sea monster, together with his two sons, as represented by this 1st-century BCE statue.

tradition was the mantic vision of divinely inspired seers and seeresses, whose ecstatic utterances were often incomprehensible to ordinary mortals. This strand, which seems to have reached Greece from the east, directly linked the classical world to earlier shamanistic traditions (see pages 10–11).

The old ways left many marks on Greek prophetic practice. The god most directly associated with the subject was Apollo, whose worship seems to have been spread through Greece by the warrior Dorians. In classical times it was Apollo's spirit that was supposed to possess seers and seeresses.

However, Apollo was a relative latecomer to the Greek pantheon, and there is evidence that his creed overlaid an earlier heritage linking foresight with the earth goddess Gaia. These chthonic origins may explain why prophecy in the classical world was often associated with caves and other underground sites, where the mysterious divinities of the soil would have been worshipped.

Oracular sites

Divinely inspired prophecy was formalized in Greece in the oracles – sacred institutions to which supplicants came for advice on what the future held. Some oracles were very ancient; besides Delphi (see pages 24–7), those at Dodona in the far north and on the Aegean island of Delos (supposedly Apollo's birth-place) were especially venerable. The Dodona oracle centred on a grove of oak trees sacred to Zeus, and its priests – described by Homer as having unwashed feet and sleeping on the ground – answered visitors' questions by interpreting the rustling of the leaves on the boughs. Later, other methods were also used: for example, priestesses sought inspiration by listening intently to the cooing of doves.

There are fairly clear indications that at other oracular sites narcotics were used to bring on the prophetic trance. At Didyma, south of Miletus in modern Turkey, the resident prophetess would inhale the fumes of boiling potions. The priestess at Colophon (now in western Turkey) swallowed a sacred draught, possibly spiked with henbane or hellebore. More sanguinary potions were also recorded: at Argos in the northeast Peloponnese, the priestess drank the blood of a sacrificial lamb, while at Aegeiria in Achaea she consumed bulls' blood, which was said to be lethal to normal mortals.

A Near-Death Experience at Levadia

The oracle of the hero Triphonios at Levadia, which lay 19 miles (30 km) due east of Delphi, was certainly one of the strangest in the classical world. The Greek traveller Pausanias described a visit there in the second century CE. Before the consultation, he bathed in a sacred river and dined on the flesh of sacrificial rams. When the time came, he was taken to drink from the waters of two springs: the Water of Lethe, to wipe away the past, and the Water of Memory, to preserve the future. Then he was taken to a 23-foot (7-m) deep chasm on the riverbank, where he had to clamber down a ladder. At the bottom, he was told to insert his legs into a fissure. When he did so, he was jerked through into darkness, receiving a painful blow to the head. Half-stunned, he heard a voice revealing the message he had come to hear, then he lost consciousness. When he came to again, he was back in the open air at the bottom of the chasm, where he was made to repeat the oracle's words. Finally he returned to the hostel nearby to fully regain his senses.

The navel of the world

The greatest of the classical oracles was the one at Delphi, on the lower slopes of Mount Parnassus in central Greece. According to the historian Diodorus Siculus, goats originally discovered the spot's sacred properties: breathing in the fumes emitted from a fissure in the ground, the animals started behaving oddly, leaping and bleating strangely. Noticing their behaviour, a goatherd went to investigate – he too became intoxicated and began uttering prophecies. Crowds soon gathered at the site, and after several people had fallen into the chasm to their deaths it was decided that it would be wisest to provide facilities for a single seeress. So a three-legged contraption referred to as the tripod was rigged up to span the gap.

Legend provided an explanation for the chasm's supernatural attributes. It was said to contain the rotting carcass of a dragon, Python, which had been sent by the jealous goddess Hera to plague Leto, who had borne children to Hera's husband Zeus. Leto's son, the god Apollo, went to Delphi to slay the monster, and thereafter the oracle was dedicated to him.

Some commentators have seen a political dimension in the myth, in that the earliest shrine at Delphi probably predated the cult of Apollo. In their view, the site was originally sacred to Gaia, Mother Earth, whose cult included the keeping of sacred serpents. From her days

An ancient Athenian red-figure vase shows Aegeus, King of Athens, consulting the Delphic oracle. The Pythia is portrayed sitting on the tripod with a laurel branch in her hand.

Delphi may have inherited the *omphalos* ("navel") – a sacred stone that was said to mark the centre of the Earth.

Prophetesses of Apollo

The prophetess at Delphi became known as the Pythia in honour of the dead Python. At first there was just one holder of the office, a virgin of noble birth. However, after a young and beautiful Pythia was abducted by a client of the oracle, there was a change of policy and only women over the age of 50 were selected. In later years these women were said to be individuals of good character chosen from the local peasantry. Some prophetesses had husbands, but they were expected to remain chaste while in office. At the height of the oracle's popularity in the sixth and fifth centuries BCE there were as many as three separate Pythias, sharing the job in rotation.

> "Begone, mother-killer!
>
> Your presence outrages me!
>
> Beware of 73!"
>
> (The Pythia's warning to Nero when he visited Delphi; he was succeeded on his assassination by the 73-year-old Galba)

By that time an elaborate ritual had developed around the business of consulting the oracle. In the early days consultations had only taken place once a year, on Apollo's birthday, but later they were instituted on the seventh day of each month, except in the three winter months, when the god was thought to travel to the far north. Supplicants were expected to leave gifts, and in time a minimum tariff was demanded that equated to about two days' wages. Cities, which often sent envoys to consult the oracle, were charged at seven times the individual rate. As the client base grew to include kings and nations from all around the classical world, Delphi became vastly wealthy, and treasuries and galleries were built to house the works of art with which the oracle was endowed.

Only men could approach the Pythia; women with questions for the oracle were expected to appoint male surrogates. The supplicant first had to make the journey to Delphi. The site itself, high up on the mountainside and backed by beetling cliffs, no doubt induced a suitable sense of awe in most visitors. At the temple complex, the newcomer was expected to purify himself with holy water. He then received a ritual cake in return for paying the consultation fee. Accompanied by a priest and often by a representative of his city (most major Greek city-states kept permanent envoys at Delphi), he then approached the temple of Apollo, where he watched as a she-goat was sacrificed. Finally, he was permitted to enter the *adyton*, or sacred precinct, where the *omphalos* was kept. There, behind a screen, the Pythia was waiting.

This Greek marble statue representing the reclining figure of the Pythia was crafted in the 5th century BCE, at a time when kings from around the Greek world sent envoys to consult the Delphic oracle.

> "Bright Apollo no longer has a roof over his head, a prophetic laurel or a babbling spring. Yes, even the murmuring water has dried up."
>
> (The Pythia, describing the state of the oracle in 362ce, near the end of its life)

The Pythia in her turn had prepared herself for her sacred duties. On days when she was to prophesy, she purified herself by fasting and by bathing in the Castalian spring, not far from the temple. She too was present while a she-goat was sacrificed, this one in the *adyton* itself. She then drank from another sacred stream, inhaled the fumes of burning barley meal and laurel in the precinct, and was given some laurel leaves to chew. These have generally been taken to come from *Laurus nobilis*, the familiar bay leaves of modern kitchens, but there are also toxic laurel genera, and it is possible that one of these was used, to narcotic effect. Finally the Pythia took up her position on the tripod — still supposedly located above the mantic fissure, although archeological evidence in fact suggests that the site of the temple had been moved — and there she entered her prophetic trance.

The words of the Pythia

The Pythia's utterances were often rambling and incoherent, and in themselves might have meant little to questioners. Her words were noted down by attendant priests, and it was these men who interpreted their meaning and produced a written response, often in verse. One copy was given to the supplicant; another, engraved on stone, was kept in the temple archives. Obviously this gave the priests a large measure of editorial control over the prophetess's pronouncements — as a result, the priests were very much a part of the prophetic process. Most were men of learning (the historian Plutarch held the post in the first century CE)

and they went to considerable lengths to keep themselves well informed. There was even a pigeon-post service that brought news of current events across Greece to Delphi soon after they happened. Careful intelligence thus combined with prophetic inspiration to maintain the shrine's reputation.

Both elements no doubt played a part in the story of Croesus, the legendarily wealthy ruler of Lydia (in what is now Turkey), and his dealings with the oracle in the sixth century BCE. Alarmed by the rising power of neighbouring Persia under its dynamic young ruler Cyrus, Croesus mooted the idea of a preventive strike. However, fearing to act without knowing the consequences of his move, he sent envoys to no fewer than seven oracles scattered around the classical world. To determine which one to believe, he devised a test: the seers were asked to specify what the king himself would be doing at a given time. The Pythia was the only one to give the correct answer: boiling lamb and tortoise flesh in a bronze vessel.

wooden walls at salamis

Among the most politically sensitive messages ever delivered at Delphi was the advice given to emissaries from Athens in 480BCE at the time of the Persian invasion of Greece (see page 63). At first the Pythia advised Athenians to flee the city, which must inevitably be destroyed by King Xerxes's huge army. When the envoys insisted on a second consultation, she offered slightly more constructive guidance, recommending that they should entrust their safety to wooden walls, and concluding by stating that Salamis, the "divine island", would destroy the children of women either in the seed-time or the harvest. Taking counsel, the Athenians decided that her words meant that they should confront the Persians in a naval battle in the narrow strait between Salamis, an offshore island in the Saronic Gulf, and the city. They did so, and won a famous victory. Subsequently Xerxes's army was destroyed, and Greece was never again threatened by the Persians.

The remains of the Tholos temple at the Sanctuary of Athena Pronaia, the gateway to the main temple complex at Delphi. Built in the early 4th century BCE, the Tholos has an unusual circular shape. This may represent the sacred forest groves of the chthonic religion that is thought to predate the oracle itself.

Convinced by the accuracy of the Pythia's reply, Croesus sent again for her advice on his proposed military action. This time the priestess replied that if the king's forces crossed the Halys river — the stream that separated the two nations — a great empire would be destroyed. Encouraged, Croesus launched an attack and was decisively defeated. His capital, Sardis, fell to the Persians and he himself was captured. Apologists for the Pythia pointed out that her words had been strictly accurate: a great empire had indeed fallen, only it was Croesus's own.

Such ambiguity was a stock-in-trade of the Delphic seers. Plutarch himself defended it on the grounds that, as the oracle was often consulted by kings and tyrants, "to anger such men by harsh truths that went against their wishes might have been harmful for the priests". The truth of his words was tragically confirmed when the Roman emperor Nero visited the site in 67CE. When the Pythia outspokenly rebuked him for the murder of his mother Agrippina (see box, page 24), Nero retaliated by having the priests' hands and feet cut off. They were then buried alive, along with the prophetess.

The oracle falls silent

By Nero's day the oracle was already long past its prime. Plutarch recorded that in his time the oracle was rarely consulted on affairs of state, but rather dealt with "people's ordinary, day-to-day problems". Even so, it continued in use for another 200 years. Toward the end the shrine itself was in a sorry state. The temple's roof had fallen in, and the Castalian spring had been stopped, supposedly on the orders of the future emperor Hadrian. On being informed by the Pythia that he would attain the throne, Hadrian had decided that it might be imprudent to permit other aspirants to hear the same message.

The triumph of Christianity as the established faith of the Roman empire was the final straw — Christians did not approve of pagan oracles. After a thousand years, the most enduring prophetic site in the Western world was left once more to the goats who had first inhabited it.

visions of the sibyl

The legend of the Sibyl sprang up in Asia Minor, perhaps in response to influences from further east. At first it concerned a single individual known as Sibylla, who was said to have lived to a fantastic age. She had prophesied to Hecuba, queen of Troy, before the Trojan War, yet many centuries later Sibylla was still believed to be living in the city of Erythrae, opposite the island of Chios. However, in time her reputation grew so great that other sibyls appeared, and the word itself became a generic term. Initially, it was attached to freelance prophetesses who were inspired to utter predictions. In time, the established oracles determined to harness the women's prestige, and many ended up by calling on the services of a resident sibyl.

However, the best-known sibyl of antiquity was the cave-dwelling Cumaean Sibyl, who was said to write her replies to suppliants' queries on palm leaves that she laid on the floor in front of her seat. When the petitioner entered, the sea wind disordered the Sibyl's writings, and the resulting confusion was taken to symbolize our uncertain knowledge of the future.

A famous episode in Virgil's *Aeneid* describes how Aeneas visited the

Sibyl in her cave. His account details some of the procedures involved in consulting the prophetess: sacred animals had to be sacrificed, after which the prophetess was possessed by the god Apollo. Fresh light was thrown on Aeneas's subterranean

voyage when, in 1967, an English engineer named Robert Paget discovered an underground cave complex at Baia, close to Cumae. Stretching 1,100 feet (330 m) into solid rock, it included such features as an artificial watercourse that

The interior corridor in the cave of the Cumaean Sibyl located at Cumae, the site of the first Greek colony in Italy.

the sibylline oracles

The prophetic reputation of the sibyls even penetrated the Jewish and early Christian worlds. Supposedly Sibylline writings foretelling the coming of the Messiah appeared from the first century BCE on, and Christian equivalents proclaiming the approaching millennium eventually followed. The Christian texts were hugely influential in the Middle Ages, and won for the Sibyl unwonted esteem as a foreteller of Christ's birth. Her reputation as a proto-Christian received favourable mentions from some of the Church Fathers, and it survived long enough for her to appear among the sacred figures in Michelangelo's great fresco on the Sistine Chapel ceiling in the Vatican.

The Cumaean Sibyl from a detail of a tiled floor in the Duomo in Siena, Italy.

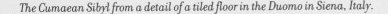

visitors had to cross in a small boat. Virgil himself may well have been familiar with the site in the first century BCE.

Rome's precious books

In Roman times the Cumaean Sibyl was remembered above all for a transaction supposed to have taken place during the reign of the last of Rome's seven kings, Tarquinius Superbus, in the sixth century BCE. The prophetess was said to have offered the monarch nine oracular books. However, Tarquinius was unwilling to pay the high price that she demanded, on which she destroyed three of the books and then proffered the remaining six for the same sum. Again the king balked at the cost, so she burned three more. Eventually, Tarquinius's augurers persuaded him that the works were too valuable to lose altogether — in the end he paid the initial asking price for the three remaining volumes.

In later years these Sibylline books were kept in a stone chest in the Temple of Jupiter on the Capitol Hill in Rome, and were among the city's most treasured possessions. The books were certainly there by 496 BCE, when they were consulted at a time of famine; subsequently their advice was sought whenever disaster threatened the city or when major political decisions needed to be taken. In 83 BCE the original books were destroyed by fire, but the outcry at the loss was so great that envoys were despatched to oracles around the Mediterranean world to gather together a replacement collection. These substitutes are last known to have been consulted in 363 CE, and are said to have still been in existence when Rome finally fell to invaders from the north a century later.

"Her colour chang'd; her face was not the same,/And hollow groans from her deep spirit came./Her hair stood up; convulsive rage possess'd/Her trembling limbs, and heav'd her labouring breast."

(THE SIBYL'S PROPHETIC FRENZY, AS DESCRIBED BY THE POET VIRGIL; TRANSLATION BY JOHN DRYDEN)

The mysteries
of pachacamac

An intriguing feature of the history of prophecy is the way in which common elements recur across different cultures and traditions. The oracle of Pachacamac in what is now Peru, once the most celebrated prophetic centre in all the Americas, could hardly be farther removed geographically from the shrine at Delphi (see pages 24–7), yet the two places had much in common.

To start with, both were sacred sites whose reputations spread across a wide region. Just as people visited Delphi from all parts of Greece, so Pachacamac, which stood not far from the site of present-day Lima, attracted suppliants in its heyday from across Peru and southern Ecuador. Both shrines were exceptionally long-lived: Delphi functioned from at least the eighth century BCE until the fourth century CE, while Pachacamac, which was certainly in use by the middle of the first millennium CE, was consulted up until the 1530s.

There were also similarities in the procedures involved in approaching the oracles. At both, suppliants had to purify themselves before they could enter the shrine. If anything, the procedures were stricter in Peru than in Greece – to visit the lowermost plaza of the temple complex, suppliants had to fast for 20 days, while to gain admission to the highest level they had to go without most foods for an entire year. Other procedures were also shared. At Pachacamac, as at Delphi, suppliants had to pay a substantial fee, although in Peru it was levied in kind in the form of cotton, textiles, maize, dried fish or, for the wealthy, gold; both shrines in consequence became legendarily rich. Each demanded animal sacrifices, with llamas and guinea pigs at Pachacamac taking the place of Delphi's slaughtered goats.

Yet there were also important differences between the two sites. To a much greater extent than Delphi, Pachacamac was the sanctuary of a god. Apollo presided at Delphi, but he had many other temples across Greece. Pachacamac was the central shrine of the creator god of that name, one of the most venerated in South America in pre-Conquest times.

The physical layouts of the two oracles were also significantly different. Delphi was very much of the earth; its inspiration came from a fissure in the ground. Following American tradition, Pachacamac reached up to the sky. The main feature of the site, which lay at the mouth of the River Lurin, was a

The cult of Pachacamac was so deeply rooted that the Incas did not dare displace it when they conquered the region in the 15th century. Instead, they incorporated it into their religion, building sanctuaries of their own around the god's temple, the pre-Incan ruins of which are pictured here.

manmade mound topped by a stepped pyramid rising almost 500 feet (150 m) above the coastal plain. The oracular shrine was at the summit, in a small sanctuary where a wooden statue of the god rested behind a curtain, hidden from the eyes of everyone but the priests.

Above all, there was no equivalent of the Delphic Pythia, or prophetess, at Pachacamac. Instead, the god's responses were passed on to suppliants by the temple priests. No indication has survived of how exactly the responses were delivered, but communication with the god was apparently private and unseen. Pachacamac lacked the high drama of the Pythia's sacred ravings; instead its continuing success rested on the enduring prestige of a corporate priesthood.

An oracle destroyed

The final fates of the two oracles were also very different. While Delphi faded away, Pachacamac's end was sudden. Seeking gold with which to pay themselves the captured Inca Atahualpa's ransom, Spanish conquistadors under the command of Francisco Pizarro's brother Hernando invaded the temple in 1533. Brushing aside the priests who tried to stop them, they broke into the sanctuary to find it almost empty; forewarned of their coming, the shrine's guardians had stripped it of its valuables. Decrying the oracle as the work of the devil, the Spaniards seized and tortured some of the priests and drove the rest from the temple. The shrine was desecrated, and the voice of Pachacamac never spoke again.

The earliest parts of the temple at Pachacamac date back to the Early Intermediate Period of Peruvian archeology (ca. 200 BCE–600 CE), when the Paracas culture, which produced woollen grave mantles such as this one, was flourishing near by.

Atahualpa's complaint

After Atahualpa, the ruler of the Incas, had been taken prisoner by Spanish conquistadors in 1532, he received a visit in captivity from the chief priest of the temple of Pachacamac. Atahualpa's Spanish captors were surprised to see that he treated his visitor with contempt. When asked why he was so angry, Atahualpa replied that the oracle had recently made three wrong predictions. It had declared that his father would recover from illness if taken out into the sun, but he had died; it had told Huascar, Atahualpa's rival in the civil war that divided the country at the time of the Spaniards' arrival, that he would be victorious; and, worst of all, it had advised Atahualpa himself to attack Pizarro's men, promising he would kill them all. The emperor was so bitter at the bad advice that he even suggested to the Spaniards that they should put the priest in chains and see if Pachacamac could free him.

The Apostle of the Third Age

The name of Joachim of Fiore means little to most people today, yet his importance is hard to exaggerate. For Professor Norman Cohn, author of *The Pursuit of the Millennium*, Joachim's was "the most influential prophetic system known to Europe until the appearance of Marxism", with its prediction of the triumph of the proletariat. However, Joachim himself could hardly have been more different from Karl Marx. Born ca. 1135, Joachim was a Cistercian monk from southern Italy. He was the abbot of a monastery for 14 years before withdrawing to lead a contemplative life until his death in 1202. Even so, his reputation as an interpreter of the Bible and as a prophet of historical development spread far even within his own lifetime. He was consulted by several popes, and King Richard I of England ("the Lionheart"), en route to the Crusades, had Joachim brought specially to Sicily so that he could interview him.

Joachim's brand of prophecy came not so much from visions as from intense biblical study. Like many of his contemporaries, he was fascinated by numerology, and he believed that the sacred numbers in the Bible – the Holy Trinity, the seven seals of the Revelation, the 12 apostles – had a deep significance. In the course of many years of research, he was granted (to judge from his writings) at least two moments of

Joachim of Fiore's vision of the monastic orders was central to the new Third Age. St Antimo monastery in Tuscany is one of countless, still active, European monasteries.

"A certain order of just men to whom it will be given to imitate perfectly the life of the son of man."

(JOACHIM OF FIORE'S PREDICTION OF A COMING MONASTIC ORDER THAT WOULD PREPARE THE WAY FOR THE THIRD AGE; MANY SAW IT FULFILLED IN THE FOUNDATION OF THE FRANCISCANS AND DOMINICANS SOON AFTER)

enlightenment, when hidden things suddenly became clear to him.

Joachim of Fiore's vision

What Joachim developed was nothing less than a new view of human history. Traditionally, the Church had had little to say about the period between Christ's First and Second Coming, at least after early hopes of an imminent apocalypse had faded (see page 21). The interval was seen essentially as a period of waiting – most churchmen were content to view it as a time of trial that had simply to be endured. However, Joachim's study of the Old and New Testaments convinced him that the Bible concealed a tale of spiritual progress. He saw the Old Testament Age of the Father as an epoch of law, obedience, hierarchy, fear and servitude, which had eventually been superseded by the New Testament Age of the Son, an era of grace, faith and filial submission. His revolutionary suggestion was that a Third Age was about to dawn that would in turn replace the Age of the Son. The new age would be the Age of the Holy Spirit, and it would be an epoch of love, freedom, contemplation, community and joy.

among them, he believed, a supreme teacher or "new leader" would arise to wean humankind from earthly things to those of the spirit. The Third Age would see the culmination of God's plan for the world — the heathen would be converted, the knowledge of God would be revealed directly to the hearts of all people, and the whole Earth would at last join in peace and ecstatic contemplation of the divine mystery.

Further study convinced Joachim that the promised time was not far away. He regarded the incubation period preparing its advent as having begun, along with the monastic movement itself, in the work of St Benedict, the sixth-century pioneer of communal religious life. Seeing a parallel with the 42 generations that, according to the Gospel of St Matthew, had separated Jesus from Abraham, Joachim believed that the Age of the Holy Spirit would dawn after a similar passage of time. In fact, according to his calculations, it would begin between the years 1200 and 1260. He also foresaw a difficult interval before its advent, which would be marked by the appearance of two new monastic orders. One of

Joachim was something of a poet as well as a mystic, and he waxed lyrical in his description of the coming time. After the starlight of the Old Testament and the dawn of the New, he wrote, the new age would be broad daylight. Similarly, it would be the summer following the other

ages' winter and spring. As a monk himself, he saw the monastic orders as the coming era's advance guard. Just as the Old Testament had had 12 patriarchs and the New the 12 apostles, so Joachim thought that 12 figures from the monastic world would mark the Third Age. From these would be purely contemplative, while the other would spread the message.

Joachim's vision of the new era struck a chord with his contemporaries, particularly in the monasteries. One precondition for the coming of the Third Age seemed to be fulfilled within a few years of his death with the foundation of the two mendicant orders, the Franciscans, dedicated to poverty and the imitation of Christ, and the preaching Dominicans. Joachim's influence was, in fact, particularly strong within these orders, especially the Franciscans whose emphasis on giving up the world for the things of the spirit chimed well with Joachim's own views.

Accusations of heresy

Joachim himself was always careful to avoid controversy, and throughout his life he enjoyed papal support. However, it was not long before some of his followers started to draw radical political conclusions from his views. Although Joachim had been a loyal supporter of the papacy, others saw the established Church, with its vast material wealth, as very much a prop of the old world that was passing. Supporters of this view started to produce commentaries on Joachim's writings, and before too long were also circulating new works in his

name. The most explosive of these collections was the "Eternal Gospel", which claimed to supersede the Old and New Testaments, rendered superfluous by the coming of the Third Age. In similar vein, the "Eternal Gospel" claimed that the

established Church had also had its day, since the messengers of truth were now the mendicant friars.

Such views were quickly condemned as heretical, and over the next century many individuals who held them were persecuted and

> "The pope ... will take possession of these areas of central Rome that he may be able the more freely and peacefully to summon his counsellors to him."
>
> (St Bridget of Sweden predicting a papal enclave in Rome, seen by some as a prevision of the Vatican City)

even killed. Greater numbers still were embroiled in controversy when the Joachite dream became enmeshed with earlier apocalyptic expectations of an Emperor of the Last Days, who was expected to usher in a golden age before Christ's Second Coming (see page 17). Now these beliefs became linked with hopes of a new figure, the Angelic Pope, who would work in conjunction with the last emperor to usher in the Age of the Holy Spirit.

Joachite ideas live on

The year 1260 came without the Third Age having dawned, but its passing did little to dent Joachim's popularity. The notion of a golden age in which all the world's faults and failings would be swept away proved simply too seductive to be easily surrendered. It lived on to influence such figures as the poet Dante – who placed Joachim among the prophets in his *Divine Comedy*.

Joachim's ideas also influenced later mystics, such as Bridget of Sweden. A mother of eight, at the age of 41 Bridget turned to a life of penance and prayer. In 1350 she travelled to Rome, where she stayed for the remaining 23 years of her life. There she saw visions predicting ruin for the Church if it did not mend its ways. She sought to pave the way for the coming of the Angelic Pope by urging the papacy to return to Rome from its temporary fourteenth-century exile in Avignon, in Provence. In similar vein, Catherine of Siena, the future patron saint of Italy, sought to redeem the Church with her visions; she saw it as the Bride of Christ disfigured in foul rags, which would one day shine forth again in beauty, bedecked with jewels and crowned with all the virtues.

Largely unrecognized, Joachim's ideas also lived on into modern times, casting their spell on generations of social reformers who saw a great age of human progress coming to sweep away the backwardness of past times. Most bizarrely of all, his theories have resurfaced in recent decades under an astrological veneer with the spread of New Age doctrines, promising in Joachite fashion a dawning era of peace, communion and love. Unlikely though it may seem, the Age of Aquarius may have endured its birth pangs more than 800 years ago in southern Italy, in the biblical musings of a shy and bookish abbot.

The sibyl of the Rhine

In medieval times, Hildegard of Bingen's name was often coupled with that of Joachim of Fiore in lists of influential prophets. An abbess and mystic from the Rhineland, Hildegard experienced visions from childhood, and in time her revelations won her a reputation that stretched across Christendom – three popes, two Holy Roman Emperors and many bishops and abbots sought her advice. Yet her vision of the Church's future was bleak. She foresaw a time when, if reform did not come, peoples and princes would forsake the Church, and its legendary wealth would shrink. Individual nations would switch their allegiance to national leaders rather than the papacy; similarly, the Holy Roman Empire itself would break up into its constituent parts. Hildegard's vision, expressed in the twelfth century, was largely borne out in the Reformation 350 years later – an ironic outcome for an abbess who herself was devotedly loyal to the Catholic Church.

The papal predictions

One of the enduring curiosities of the history of prediction are the so-called prophecies of St Malachy. The prophecies consist of a list of 111 short epithets characterizing each pope in turn from the time of Celestine II, who sat on the papal throne from 1143 to 1144. St Malachy, the supposed author, was a churchman and reformer who died in 1148. A friend of St Bernard of Clairvaux, he introduced the Cistercian order to Ireland. However, St Bernard, in his writings on the life of St Malachy, makes no mention of the prophecies. The first reference to them dates from 1595, a time when there was a vogue for papal prophecies.

The long disappearance of St Malachy's list inevitably attracted suspicion, and within a few decades of its reappearance it was being suggested that the list was a forgery. Specifically, it was said to have been created at the time of the papal election of 1590 to further the prospects of a certain Cardinal Simoncelli of Orvieto – the motto at the appropriate point in the sequence is *De antiquitate urbis*, "From the antiquity of the city", and Orvieto derives from the Latin for "old city". However, proponents of the prophecies offered an alternative explanation for its long absence. St Malachy, they claimed, had presented the list to Pope Innocent II on a visit to Rome in 1140, and it had simply got lost in the Vatican archives.

Epithets and coats of arms
Controversy about the document's authenticity continues today. Some of the earlier prophecies certainly have an appropriateness that smacks of hindsight; if not, they would have to rank as extraordinarily prescient. For example, the fifth pope on the list, Adrian IV (1154–1159), is given the motto *De rure albo*, "From the Alban country". He was the

A portrait of Pope Pius VI by Pompeo Girolamo Batoni. In St Malachy's list, Pius VI (1775–1799), who was driven into exile by Napoleon's revolutionary forces, is described as Peregrinus apostolicus, *meaning "Apostolic wanderer".*

St Peter's Square in the Vatican City, central Rome, the statelet domain of the popes named in St Malachy's famous list.

Englishman Nicholas Breakspear, who came from St Albans. Alexander IV (1254–1261), *Signium Ostiense*, was cardinal of Ostia before his election. The hermit pope Celestine V (1294) rated *Ex eremo celsus*, "The great one from the desert".

Sceptics see in such close matches prophecy after the event. More interesting, perhaps, are the predictions after 1590, which certainly postdate the list's author-ship. Many critics do see a falling off after that time, but there are still some surprisingly appropriate phrases. Benedict XV (1914–1922), whose prelacy coincided with the First World War and the militantly atheist Russian Revolution, merits *Religio depopulata*, "Religion depopulated". John Paul I, whose brief papal reign stretched for just 33 days on either side of a full moon in 1978, fits *De medietate lunae*, "From the mid-point of the moon".

Other popes can be related to their Malachite slogans through their coats of arms. Clement XIV's (1769–1774) featured a running bear, matching neatly with *Ursus velox*, "Swift bear". That of Leo XIII (1878–1903), attached to *Lumen in coelo*, "Light in the sky", showed a comet, while Paul VI's (1963–1978) – *Flos floris*, "Flower of flowers" – included a fleur-de-lys.

It is, of course, easy to exaggerate the list's accuracy by simply citing its successes. Other tags do not fit so neatly. John Paul II, the Pole who in 1978 became the first non-Italian pope for 450 years, is apostrophized as *De labore solis*, "From the labour of the sun". Attempts to find a connection by pointing out that he came from Krakow, the birthplace of Copernicus, who first expounded the Earth's solar orbit, seem forced.

Intriguingly, St Malachy's list is now close to its end. Only one motto follows John Paul's: *Gloria olivae*, "The glory of the olive". Then the sequence terminates with a fateful prediction: in the papacy of a new Peter, the Church will suffer a final persecution, after which Rome itself will be destroyed and the Last Judgment will come.

"In the last persecution of the Holy Roman church there shall reign Peter the Roman, who will feed the sheep amid great tribulations; and when these are passed, the city of the seven hills will be utterly destroyed and the terrible judge will judge the people."

(ST MALACHY'S PREDICTION OF THE LAST POPE, WHO WILL BE APPOINTED DURING THE TWENTY-FIRST CENTURY)

the voices of joan of arc

A painting by Gillot Saint-Evre (ca. 1833) depicts Joan of Arc before King Charles VII, whom she begged to allow her to lead the French forces against the English. It was only after intense ecclesiastical questioning that Joan was allowed to join the army.

Few stories in history are more astonishing than that of Joan of Arc, known as the Maid of Orléans. In 1429, at a time when France's fortunes in the Hundred Years War with England were at their lowest ebb, an illiterate peasant girl who saw visions of angels managed to gain an introduction to the king of France. In just a few days she persuaded him that she could boost the morale of his flagging forces. Sent to Orléans, which was under siege by the English, Joan succeeded in freeing the city and driving off the attacking army in just nine days. She then fulfilled a pledge to take the king across enemy-held land to the city of Rheims (where French kings were traditionally crowned) for his coronation, which had been delayed for more than six years by the English occupation. Soon after, Joan fell into enemy hands and was accused of heresy and witchcraft. Condemned by French bishops in collusion with the English, she was burned at the stake in 1431, still not yet 20 years old. The

charges against Joan of Arc were posthumously revoked, and almost 500 years later, in 1920, the Church declared her a saint.

Joan's prophetic gift took the form of voices, which she first heard at the age of 13. They belonged to St Michael, St Catherine and St Margaret – the three patron saints of the district of eastern France from which Joan came. The voices told her to go to the king and offer her services – no easy task in the war-torn France of her day. That she persuaded the local military commander to send her, in male disguise, with an escort and a recommendation to Charles VII was in itself little short of a miracle.

Several episodes in Joan's story suggest that she possessed clairvoyance. When she first entered the royal presence, the king deliberately hid himself among his courtiers to test her powers, yet she went straight to him without hesitation. She also reportedly received her battle sword as the result of a vision – her voices

> "the king of heaven sends me to you with the message that you shall be anointed and crowned in the city of rheims. will you believe that i am sent by god?"
>
> (JOAN OF ARC TO KING CHARLES VII OF FRANCE, AT THEIR FIRST MEETING IN 1429)

Joan of Arc at King Charles VII's coronation, as portrayed by Jean Auguste Dominique Ingres in 1854. With her advance guard, Joan — clad in white armour and flying her own standard — had already freed the city of Orléans. Yet she subsequently failed to persuade the king to undertake further military exploits, notably the liberation of Paris.

instructed her to send word to the church authorities in the village of Fierbois, telling them to look under the altar. Sure enough, they found a rusty blade in an ancient chest. Polished up, the sword provided Joan with a brand with which to lead her forces into combat. It was also claimed of Joan that she once gave word of a French defeat 185 miles (300 km) away, two days before news of it first reached the neighbourhood.

The Maid of Kent

An English prophetess whose story bears some parallels to that of Joan of Arc was Elizabeth Barton, the Maid of Kent. A domestic servant, she too heard voices and saw visions. The Maid first began to prophesy in 1525 at the age of 19, after an illness. Word of her visions reached the Archbishop of Canterbury, who sent two monks to examine her. One, Edward Bocking, became convinced that she was indeed inspired by the Virgin Mary, and took her to a nunnery in Canterbury. However, the times were troubled — the Protestant Reformation was under way on the Continent, and in England King Henry VIII was mooting the divorce that would ultimately lead him to break with Rome. The Maid was fiercely loyal to the Catholic Church, and her prophecies took on an increasingly political tone. She even predicted that Henry would die if the divorce went ahead. Word of the Maid's claims eventually reached King Henry VIII, who ordered that she should be arrested. Investigated by the Church authorities, she agreed to recant, but even so the king demanded her death. She was hanged at Tyburn, along with Bocking and four other supporters, in 1534.

At her trial, Joan was asked to explain something that mystified many: namely, why she could not foresee, and therefore avoid, her own capture. She replied that her voices had indeed warned her that she would be taken before Midsummer's Day (the actual date fell in mid-May) but had refused to name the day. At her trial she continued to prophesy final victory for France, insisting that the English would eventually lose all their cross-Channel possessions. Her claims were duly borne out. However, it could be argued that, thanks to the boost Joan had given to national morale, the result she foresaw was actually of her own making.

The Blood-stained path to Heavenly peace

Like the West, China has a tradition of millenarian revolutionaries who have promised to create a paradise on Earth in times of crisis. None did so to more cataclysmic effect than Hong Xiuquan, whose attempt to create the Heavenly Kingdom of Great Peace – in Chinese, the Taiping Tianguo – devastated much of central China in the mid-nineteenth century and left an estimated 20 million people dead.

Hong was born into a poor family from southern China, near the port of Canton. His parents had hopes that he would succeed in the highly competitive civil-service examinations that were the route to success at the time. However, Hong repeatedly failed the test. After a third unsuccessful attempt, he suffered a breakdown while returning to his village and was delirious for several days. In his exhausted state he experienced visions that were to remain in his memory for years.

Hong saw himself in the presence of a bearded man in a black dragon robe and a high-brimmed hat whom he was told was his father. The father complained that he had given life to the peoples of the Earth, but they had been led astray by devils. Seeking redress, he gave Hong a sword and a golden seal. Hong then set to work to drive out the demons, while his elder brother held the seal aloft, blinding the demons with its light. Once the foe was vanquished Hong was welcomed back to Heaven, where his father gave him moral instruction before charging him to return to Earth to accomplish a similar cleansing mission.

Hong eventually regained his health and went back to his village, where he worked as a schoolmaster.

This painting, dated 1760, depicts a Qing warrior similar to those sent to suppress the Taiping rebels less than a century later.

It was only six years later that he chanced upon a moral tract written by a Christian missionary and entitled *Good Words for Exhorting the Age*. Reading this work changed Hong's life. He immediately saw in the Christian religion an explanation of his mysterious vision. The father, he now realized, was the Christian God, and the elder brother who had helped him fight the demons was Jesus Christ. He himself, then, was God's younger son, and he had been entrusted with a sacred mission: not just to bring Christianity to China,

> "My hand grasps
> the killing power
> in Heaven and
> earth;/To behead
> the evil ones, spare
> the just and ease the
> people's sorrow."
>
> (LINES FROM A POEM COMPOSED BY
> HONG XIUQUAN IN A TRANCE STATE
> DURING HIS ORIGINAL VISION)

but also to sweep out the devils who held the nation in their grip.

Inspired, Hong set out to spread the word. His inflammatory message fell on receptive ears. The Qing dynasty ruling China at the time was deeply unpopular. The nation had grown backward and impoverished. Worse still, it had recently suffered defeat at the hands of the British in the First Opium War of 1839–1842, and foreigners were busy carving out lucrative trading concessions in the major ports and cities.

The Taiping rebels

Hong soon attracted a following, chiefly among the poor, but also among disaffected students, as well as farmers and businessmen crippled by taxes. In 1851 his supporters captured the southern town of Yongan. From this base Hong declared himself the "Heavenly King" and announced his intention to conquer China and exterminate all idolaters.

In 1853 Hong's forces captured Nanjing. The Taiping rebels were by now half a million strong, and it seemed Hong was well on the way to fulfilling his ambition, the more so when, from 1856 on, the Qing dynasty became embroiled in a second opium war with Britain.

There was little Christian charity about Hong's rule, however. He forbade alcohol, tobacco and prostitution, and punished rape, adultery and opium-smoking with death. Gradually disaffection with the puritanical Heavenly Kingdom spread. When rivals to Hong emerged in the leadership of the movement, he had them murdered. A northern expedition sent to capture Beijing ended in defeat. Yet, ironically, the force that finally did most to bring the Kingdom to an end was that of the Western Christian powers, who were concerned at the threat that the rebels presented to their trading concessions. A combined host of European mercenaries and imperial troops under a talented British officer, General Charles Gordon, turned the tide of the conflict. The rebels were driven back to their base of Nanjing.

Hong died on 1 June 1864 and the besieged city fell six weeks later. After its collapse, the surviving rebels were largely exterminated by a vengeful government. The Heavenly Kingdom of Great Peace came to an end in a welter of bloodshed.

Subjected to tight discipline, Hong's ragtag army proved amazingly successful. Here a detail of a Chinese print shows the Taiping rebels attacking the city of Nanjing, a former capital of China. Once the city had been taken in 1853, Hong's forces slaughtered the entire Qing garrison together with their families — in all some 25,000 people.

joseph smith, the Latter-Day prophet

In 1847 Brigham Young, Joseph Smith's successor as head of the Church of Jesus Christ of the Latter-Day Saints, led his followers to a new home in Utah, where Smith's work finally took root. Salt Lake City, the settlement founded by the Mormon pioneers, is now the world capital of the Mormon faith. This 19th-century print shows the nascent city on the shores of Great Salt Lake.

Some prophecy stories are universal, but the truly extraordinary saga of Joseph Smith, the founder of the Mormon faith, could only have happened in one place at one time: the USA in the early nineteenth century. Throughout his life, Smith experienced disasters that in crowded Europe or Asia would have finished his career, but in America at that time he could simply move on.

Born in 1805, Smith grew up in western New York State in unsettled times. The War of Independence was a recent memory, and the young nation it had created was still struggling to find its identity. Smith's home region, in particular, was swept by waves of religious revivalism.

In 1823, at the age of 17, Smith announced that an angel named Moroni had appeared to him as he was praying in his bedroom, and had told him that he had been chosen to restore God's church on Earth. Four years later, on a nearby hill, the angel delivered to Smith golden tablets inscribed in an unknown script said to be "reformed Egyptian". Along with the tablets were two stones, called Urim and Thummim, that magically bestowed on Smith the ability to translate the language.

The result of Smith's efforts, published in 1830, was the *Book of Mormon*, which described the fate of the lost tribes of Israel that had, it claimed, emigrated to America in the centuries before Christ. As the prophet of this new revelation, Smith was also granted the rights of apostolic priesthood, giving him divine authority to set up and run a church to spread the message.

> "There was a book deposited, written upon gold plates .... also there were two stones in silver bowls ... the possession and use of these stones were what constituted 'seers' in former times."
>
> (JOSEPH SMITH DESCRIBING THE REVELATION OF THE *BOOK OF MORMON*, AND THE MAGICAL TOOLS SUPPLIED FOR TRANSLATING IT)

Tall and good-looking, Smith was also a fluent and persuasive speaker, and he soon attracted support for his seemingly unlikely claims. News of the American prophet spread rapidly. Within a year of establishing a first church at Fayette in New York, he also had a base in Ohio, to which he soon moved. Yet from the start his claims also aroused hostility: as early as 1832, he was stripped, tarred and feathered by an angry mob.

Within five years the Ohio community ran into financial difficulty. The church had accumulated debts through buying property that even the contributions pouring in from the faithful could not cover. To bridge the gap, Smith set up a bank that failed (it was one of many to do so in the US banking crisis of 1837). Smith himself was put on trial and fined. He decided to move on.

By this time another Mormon community had sprung up in Missouri, and had already suffered persecution from "gentiles" – non-Mormon residents – who feared they would be swamped by the sect's followers. Smith's arrival, along with that of many more believers, only exacerbated existing tensions, leading to open hostilities in 1838. Faced with the prospect of further bloodshed, Smith opted for another move, this time to Illinois, where he established the town of Nauvoo as a third attempt to create an American Zion, or heavenly settlement.

The harsh treatment the Mormons had suffered in Missouri – one massacre had killed 17 of the faithful – had generated some sympathy for their cause, and at first they received a friendly welcome in their new home. But the same fears and tensions soon arose there too as thousands of new settlers swarmed into the area. Events came to a head in 1844, when Smith declared his candidacy for the US presidency. Attacked by dissidents within Nauvoo itself, he had the press on which their newspaper was printed destroyed. Arrested on the orders of the governor of Illinois, Smith was held for questioning with three companions. But the jail where they were kept was attacked by hostile militiamen, and in the ensuing fracas Joseph Smith (himself armed with a revolver) was shot dead, along with his brother Hyrum. Ironically, Smith's death at "gentile" hands in the long run did much to establish the Mormon faith – like many prophets before him, he had become a martyr in his own cause.

vision of the promised land

Inspired by their late leader Joseph Smith, the Mormon faithful continued the trek in search of their promised land, led by Brigham Young. In July 1847 Young took a small group up a mountain from which they had a commanding view of the Salt Lake valley laid out below. Young declared it the chosen place, and he claimed that he had had a vision in Nauvoo in which Smith had shown him this very mountain and instructed him to build their perfect society in its shadow. Ensign Peak, as it is known, stands just north of the modern city.

An engraving of Joseph Smith published in 1894.

Native American Holy Men

In June 1876, the Lakota Sioux chief and visionary Sitting Bull went to the foot of a precipitous rock outcrop in the Powder River country of central Montana in search of a vision. A crisis was facing his people, the western branch of the Sioux nation. The US government had despatched troops to force the Sioux from their ancestral hunting grounds onto a reservation set aside for them in South Dakota. The 45-year-old chief needed guidance on how best to respond. He went to the hills to pray.

The conclusion that Sitting Bull drew from his vigil was that he should perform the Sun Dance, the holiest of Sioux rituals. First he cut 50 notches in his flesh, offering up the "scarlet blanket" of self-sacrifice to the Sky Spirit. Then the chief danced continuously in the open air for more than 24 hours, until he finally collapsed from exhaustion. And in his stupor he was granted the revelation that he sought. He saw white soldiers falling from the sky "like grasshoppers" into his camp.

It was the sign that Sitting Bull had been waiting for. Soon after, the Sioux and their Cheyenne allies defeated Lieutenant Colonel George Armstrong Custer's US cavalry force by the Little Bighorn river and won a famous victory. The great chief's vision had been confirmed.

Sitting Bull's triumph was a rare positive moment in the generally sad history of the Native American struggle against encroaching white settlement. A feature of that long-drawn-out tragedy was the

Lakota Sioux men who had experienced powerful and sacred visions, men such as Sitting Bull (left), belonged to fraternal dream societies. To be a member gave one influence and conferred great honour, but it also carried with it an obligation to act selflessly for the well-being of the people.

A contemporary ledger drawing by Amos Bad Heart Buffalo of the Sioux tribe shows the opening of the Battle of Little Bighorn.

appearance of a succession of visionary religious leaders who claimed to have a special message from the spirit world that could, if certain conditions were met, stop the long retreat of their peoples and restore a hunter-gatherer golden age. It was, by and large, white men who gave these individuals the title of "prophets", drawing an obvious parallel with the Old Testament divines. Yet the word worked in another sense too, for all the individuals concerned drew on a long tradition of trance-induced visions, derived ultimately from

Siberian shamans (see pages 10–11) and brought to America at some distant point in the past over the Bering Strait land-bridge from Asia.

Prophets from north and south

The first Native American figure to earn the name was Popé, a Pueblo medicine man who led a revolt against Spanish settlers in what is now New Mexico. Popé's example was seminal in several ways. His movement, which was supported by almost all the Pueblo tribes, began in reaction to proselytizing activities by Spanish missionaries that seemed to threaten traditional beliefs and customs. He thought that he was acting in response to instructions from the ancestral spirits of his people – in his case, the sacred *kachinas*, mythical beings who revisit the Earth each winter. Popé's goal was to restore the status quo that had existed in the past, and for a time he succeeded – in August 1680 he drove the settlers from Santa Fe.

The end of the story also proved sadly typical: Popé was deposed by his own people, and Spanish rule was re-established over the area shortly after his death in 1692.

Much further north, the Delaware produced a string of prophets through the second half of the eighteenth century in response to increased white encroachment on their lands. The best known of these figures were Neolin, who helped the Ottawa chief Pontiac in his attack on Detroit in 1763, and Wangomend, actually a Munsee Indian, who took his message to the Ohio Indians.

Like Popé, the Delaware prophets had visions and sought primarily to inspire their people – predicting the future was incidental to their message. Their view of the future usually harked back to an idyllic time before the white men had come to America. Ironically, though, the prophets borrowed some ideas from Christian missionaries – Wangomend was influenced by the Moravian Brethren.

"you ask me to plow the ground. shall I take a knife and tear my mother's bosom? then, when I die, she shall not take me to her bosom to rest."

(SMOHALLA, THE WANAPUM DREAMER, EXPOUNDING HIS REVELATION THAT HIS PEOPLE SHOULD NOT HARM MOTHER EARTH THROUGH AGRICULTURE)

Tenskwatawa's dream

As the wave of white settlement pressed westward, the Delawares' mantle passed to the Shawnee peoples, who produced a significant prophet of their own in Tenskwatawa, or "Open Door", the brother of the great political leader Tecumseh. For the first 37 years of his life Tenskwatawa lived very much in his brother's shadow as a rather dissolute medicine man with a weakness for alcohol. Then, in 1805, in a time of epidemic, Tenskwatawa had a dream. In it he saw himself on the road taken by souls after death. The path branched, and he followed the broader track. It led to a house called Eternity. This was a place of punishment, where he could hear souls in torment "roaring like the falls of a river".

Even though Tenskwatawa was no Christian, the imagery would have been familiar to any missionary. Priests could also have supported the message that he drew from his vision, for he preached a strict moral code, banning alcohol – which he now abandoned – along with polygamy, violence against women and children, fornication and dishonesty. Most startlingly of all, he urged his followers to throw away their traditional medicine bags – the bundles of talismans that were their most sacred possessions – as a symbol of their desire to start a new life.

Tenskwatawa's vision of the future, though, was firmly in the native tradition. A time was coming,

"when the sun died, i went up to heaven and saw god and all the people who had died a long time ago. god told me to come back and tell my people they must be good and love one another, and not fight, or steal, or lie."

(Wovoka, the Ghost Dance prophet, describing his vision of 1 January 1889, during a solar eclipse)

he claimed, when the Great Spirit would sweep across the land, darkening it for two days. Afterward, the whites would be gone, buried alongside the Native American peoples who had failed to change their lives. Then the Spirit would release the lost game animals from the place where they had been hidden, and the virtuous would repossess the land. The promised time was just a few years away.

For almost seven years, Tenskwatawa attracted thousands of followers from across the Midwest to his village, known to the whites as Prophetstown. Then he met disaster. In 1811 US troops approached Prophetstown while his brother was away, and Tenskwatawa encouraged the warriors gathered there to launch a preemptive attack, promising them invulnerability. The white soldiers' gunpowder, he said, would be turned to sand.

The attack, which became known as the Battle of the Tippecanoe River, was not a success, and relatives of the fighters who were killed turned on Tenskwatawa, blaming him for the defeat. Although they subsequently released him unharmed, his reputation had been damaged beyond repair and he never exerted much influence again.

Dancing in despair

The situation of Native Americans continued to deteriorate throughout the nineteenth century, stimulating a further round of apocalyptic dreams, now centred on mystical dances. One such movement surfaced in Christianized form among the Flathead and Nez Percé tribes in the 1820s. Then, 30 years later, the Wanapum medicine man Smohalla introduced the Washat dance as the focus of resistance to attempts by the US government to turn the northwestern tribespeople into farmers. So intense was Smohalla's hostility to agriculture that he refused to cut grass – the

Earth Mother's hair – or dig the soil that was her skin (see box, page 45).

The so-called Prophet Dances climaxed in the Ghost Dance movement associated with the Paiute shaman Wovoka. In 1889, ill and delirious, he had a vision in which he saw the existing world destroyed by a great flood. In its place would arise a new world, peopled by tribesmen both living and dead, whose spirits would fly there on magic wings. In the new world they would once more follow the old ways.

News of Wovoka's vision spread at a time when Native Americans' fortunes were at a low ebb. The railway, far from bringing the spirits of dead Native Americans

as Wodziwob had hoped (see box, below), had in fact brought a new tide of white settlers, so there was a receptive audience for Wovoka's message. He taught that his followers could help bring on the promised time by practising a strict morality and reviving the circular dance popularized by Wodziwob. White observers called it the Ghost Dance, as it was expected to raise the dead.

For a time Wovoka's dream gripped the imagination of a people close to despair. All the way from southern California to the Dakotas, groups gathered to perform the shuffling dance, moving slowly clockwise round a central fire in imitation of the sun while chanting

sacred songs. But the hopes the movement raised were not to be realized. Instead, they received a fatal blow when a group of Sioux who had gathered to practise the dance at Wounded Knee creek in the Badlands of South Dakota were fired on by panicking soldiers in 1890.

Like the other Prophet Dance movements that had preceded it, the Ghost Dance revival petered out in the wake of the massacre at Wounded Knee. The Native American prophets had raised their voices in response to a real and desperate need, but in the long run the considerable forces ranged against them had simply been too much for their visionary powers to overcome.

wodziwob's vision

The origins of the Native American Ghost Dance (see main text, above) date back to 1869, when a medicine man from the Paiute tribe named Wodziwob had a vision. The transcontinental railway spanning the USA had just been completed, and in his dream Wodziwob saw a train approaching filled with recently dead tribesmen who had been miraculously revived. Their appearance, Wodziwob believed, would trigger an upturn in Native American fortunes. Meanwhile, he urged, his people should pave the way by practising an ancient dance that had fallen into disuse; circular in form, it symbolized the progress of the sun across the sky. For a time Wodziwob attracted a considerable following, but when the promised deliverance failed to come his support fell away.

The stars and animals decorating this Arapaho Ghost Dance dress represent the spirits of ancestors and natural forces, whose support the dancer enlisted in an attempt to bring back order to the cosmos.

The secrets of fatima

On 13 May 1917, three children were watching sheep near the village of Fatima in central Portugal when something remarkable happened. They saw a bright light above the branches of an oak tree; in it, the figure of a lady appeared. She spoke to the children, telling them not to be afraid and promising to return in a month's time.

The children described what they had seen to their parents, who were sceptical. Nevertheless word spread, and on 13 June about 50 people followed the children to the hollow. The lady appeared once more to the children, promising to return again. The onlookers did not see her, but spoke of observing a bright cloud.

Some 500 people turned up on 13 July, when the lady, who had by now identified herself as the Virgin Mary, delivered a revelation to the children that was kept secret for many years.

A contemporary photograph of the three shepherd children, aged ten, nine and seven, who saw the extraordinary vision at Fatima.

She also said that she would appear three more times, and that at her final appearance in October she would deliver a sign.

News of the visions continued to spread, and when the time for the August visitation came round, the local authorities took the children into custody to prevent a public disturbance. However, the children saw the lady again after their release, and she once more repeated her promise for October.

By that time word of the expected miracle had reached the national press, and on the promised day at least 50,000 people assembled. Among the witnesses were several doubting journalists. The day had been rainy, but by the appointed time the sky cleared. When it did so, the crowd saw the sun turn silver as if in a fog. The sun then performed what one editor described as "a macabre dance", whirling like a top and then seeming to spiral down toward the Earth before retreating again. Meanwhile, there were odd visual phenomena at ground level – witnesses spoke of the light turning first deep blue and then yellow.

The purpose of this display, witnessed as far as 6 miles (10 km) away, was apparently to lend credence to the message that the lady had delivered on 13 July. At the time the children merely let it be known that she had asked that a chapel be built for her and that people pray for peace. Subsequently, however, Lucia dos Santos, the eldest of the three children – the other two both died of influenza within a couple of years of the

"when you see a night illumined by an unknown light, know that this is the great sign given you by god that he is about to punish the world for its crimes, by means of war, famine and persecutions of the church and of the holy father."

(THE FATIMA PROPHECY PREDICTING THE OUTBREAK OF THE SECOND WORLD WAR)

Pilgrims kneel at the Shrine of Our Lady at Fatima, ca. 1949. The shrine was erected in the cove where the children first reported seeing the vision of the Virgin Mary in 1917.

New York Times covered the story with the headline "Aurora Borealis Startles Europe – People Flee in Fear".

The third part of the revelation remained under wraps in the Vatican until it was published in 2000. It turned out to be another vision. The three children had seen a man robed in white whom they recognized as the pope leading a crowd of believers up a steep hill. At the top the pilgrims reached a rough-hewn cross. As they knelt to pray beneath it, they were mown down by soldiers in a hail of bullets and arrows.

In releasing the prophecy, John Paul II made it clear that he saw its fulfilment in the attempt made on his own life in 1981. The attack, apparently carried out at the instigation of Eastern-bloc security services, took place in Rome on 13 May – 64 years to the day after the Lady first appeared. On his recovery John Paul in fact travelled to Fatima to give thanks for his deliverance, leaving one of the bullets fired at him in the great Catholic shrine that now dominates the village. Two years later he performed a service consecrating Russia to the Virgin, as the Lady had requested. Believers like to point out that less than 12 months later Mikhail Gorbachev came to power in the USSR and the process of dismantling the old, anti-religious Soviet system got under way.

visitation – wrote down further details of what they had seen. These accounts, prepared in 1936, 1942 and 1944 and delivered in sealed envelopes to church authorities, contained the raw material of the famous "secrets of Fatima".

A triple revelation

According to Lucia, the Lady first revealed to the children a vision of Hell as a sea of flames. Then she gave them a message. She said that the First World War, which was raging at the time, would soon end, but that if people continued to offend God a second war would break out within the pontificate of the next pope. The sign of the war's coming would be a strange light in the night. To prevent

further evil, the Lady asked that Russia – shortly to be taken over by the militantly atheistic Bolsheviks – should be consecrated to her and certain Catholic rituals carried out. If this was done, she said, Russia would in time be converted and there would be world peace.

The next pope was in fact Pius XI, who died in January 1939, just before the outbreak of the Second World War. Lucia, who subsequently became a nun and who is still alive at the time of writing at the age of 95, explained the slight discrepancy by insisting that the war had actually begun with Hitler's invasion of Austria in 1938. Six weeks before that event, there was indeed a strange light in the sky, one that caused global comment. The

Dreams and premonitions

From early on, dreams have been seen as pathways to hidden knowledge. For many cultures they were channels to the world of the spirits – mighty beings who could, if they chose, use their powers to grant dreamers foreknowledge. Similar notions have survived into recent times, though long stripped of their earlier, animistic underpinnings. Instead, modern interpretations tend to follow Freud in stressing the dreaming mind's ability to access the subconscious. Premonitory dreams, in this view, can, like waking premonitions, provide occasional intuitive glimpses of the future beyond the reach of the rational mind.

Often the revelations are purely personal; thousands, if not millions, of individuals around the world claim to have had advance visions of their future partners or the deaths of loved ones in this way. But there is also a long tradition of presentiments of traumatic public events. People have claimed to have had forebodings of the assassinations of political leaders since at least the time of Julius Caesar. Another hotspot seems to be travel disasters; previsions of major air and rail crashes are legion, while whole books have been written about claimed precognitions of the sinking of the *Titanic*.

the gods of mesopotamia

The story of premonitory dreams begins in Mesopotamia, the land that lies between the rivers Tigris and Euphrates in what is now Iraq. It was in Sumer, the birthplace of the region's earliest civilization, that the art of writing first emerged.

As in Egypt, the people of the Mesopotamian states worshipped multiple gods – between three and four thousand, according to most reckonings. Some of the major divinities represented elemental forces, such as Enlil, god of the wind and storms, and Enki, god of waters. Other deities were associated with places; one such was Marduk, who was the god of Babylon. Eventually, as Babylon came to dominate the other city-states in the region,

Marduk became Mesopotamia's chief god.

Contacting the deities

There were several channels through which the Mesopotamians could communicate with their gods. City-states built dwellings for the deities in the form of ziggurats resembling manmade mountains. In the shrines that topped these huge structures, statues of the divinities were dressed and feted, and food offerings were left each day to sustain them. Although only the priests had direct access to these images, ordinary worshippers could still seek to win divine favour by leaving votive offerings, hoping to be rewarded with health, long life and prosperity.

An Akkadian cylinder-seal impression dating from ca. 2300 BCE shows Gilgamesh, hero of the Mesopotamian Epic of Gilgamesh, and his companion Enkidu. The pair are depicted killing the Bull of Heaven and other monsters.

There were also more direct means of discovering the will of these multifarious divinities. Mesopotamians paid great heed to omens, pioneering various forms of divination, including the inspection of animals' livers for telltale lumps and marks. Divination was even given a royal pedigree – it was traced back to a legendary ruler of Sumer, Ednmeduranki, said to have lived before the great flood of Sumerian myth. Diviners studied each

Mesopotamian monarch's prospects particularly closely. If the signs were bad, it was not unknown for a king to abdicate temporarily, handing over the throne to a substitute who, at the end of the appointed time, would be killed, taking the predicted wrath of the gods with him to the grave.

In this god-ridden world, those who could analyse dreams held high positions. The reading of dreams was regarded as a job requiring expertise – dream books were assembled, and a special class of priests emerged to interpret them.

commissioned in a dream

One of the oldest surviving Sumerian texts comprises 1,363 lines of cuneiform writing on two 12-inch (30-cm) high cylinders. The text describes how the governor of the city-state of Lagash set about restoring the temples of the town of Girsu in response to a command received in a dream. According to the inscription, Gudea, who ruled Lagash around the year 2140BCE, was sleeping when Ningirsu, god of the town, came to him and told him: "You will build a house for me; let me give you the sign, let me tell of my rites in accordance with the holy stars". The god even conveyed a plan of the temple he wished to have built; it survives in outline, cradled in the lap of a seated statue of the ruler that is now in the Louvre Museum in Paris.

In Mesopotamian literature, sleep-induced premonitions play an unusually important role. Some of the most powerful images in the Mesopotamian myths have a dream-like quality: for example, the flight of the deified shepherd-king Etana on an eagle's back in quest of the herb of rejuvenation. More directly, one version of the myth of the god Dumuzi – who is doomed, like Persephone in Greek myth, to spend six months of each year in the underworld – describes how he dreams his own fate, hunted down by the death-demons known as *galla*s. Forewarned, Dumuzi uses all his ingenuity to escape, but to no avail. The moral of the tale is that death comes for everyone, no matter what steps they take to prevent it.

The Epic of Gilgamesh

In Mesopotamia's great classic, the Epic of Gilgamesh, many of the main steps of the unfolding action are foretold at length in dreams. Gilgamesh, ruler of the city-state of Uruk, has two symbolic presages of his meeting with the wild man Enkidu, initially his rival and later his boon companion. The first sign comes when Gilgamesh sees a thunderbolt falling to earth, and then a copper axe – symbols interpreted by his mother, the goddess Ninsun, as representing a man of great strength whom he will learn to love. Later, dreams warn Gilgamesh of the dangers posed by the forest monster Huwawa, while Enkidu foresees his own final sickness, warning his companion,

An 8th-century BCE Assyrian stone relief portrays the Mesopotamian hero Gilgamesh holding a lion that he has captured.

"Oh my brother, they are taking me away from you". Enkidu's vision is one of the first surviving records of a death foretold, and it strikes a note of fatalism that runs as a leitmotif through Mesopotamian culture. In the words of one text summing up the human condition: "The gods alone live forever under the divine sun; but as for humankind, their days are numbered, and all their activities will be nothing but wind".

foretelling
pharaoh's future

Through dreams, the Egyptians believed, the gods – such as the falcon-headed sky god Horus, pictured here – could make direct contact with human beings. People sometimes even slept within temple compounds in the hope of receiving a prophetic dream from a god.

For Egyptians in pharaonic times, the unseen world of gods and spirits was as real as the one in which they earned their living. Aware of their own vulnerability in the face of an uncertain fate, they sought in various ways to ensure that their actions were in tune with these invisible powers. One way of avoiding unnecessary risk was to consult the calendars of lucky and unlucky days that were an enduring part of Egyptian life. Another involved scanning dreams for portents that might give advance warning of triumphs or trouble to come.

Dreams were considered to be "revelations of truth", in the words of one Middle Kingdom text, the *Instructions of King Amenhemat I*. There is also evidence that dreams were sometimes regarded as objective glimpses of a higher reality – so much so that their significance was not limited to the dreamer alone.

Dream books
People often sought help in unravelling the meaning of their dreams. In a land where the vast majority of people was illiterate, priests with an understanding of the written word enjoyed high status. Among the texts the so-called "lector" (literate) priests could consult were dream books, which claimed to explain the meaning of different dream images.

One such text has survived, in an incomplete form, in a manuscript dating from the twelfth century BCE. Interestingly, it gives two different readings according to the personality type of the dreamer: one for votaries of the beneficent god Horus, thought of as calm and equable individuals, and the other for followers of the divine trouble-maker, the intemperate Seth.

Some of the interpretations accord with those that might be offered today: dreaming of plunging into a river, for example, meant purification from evil. Others are more enigmatic: for a man to dream of making love to a woman was inauspicious, foretelling mourning, while seeing an ostrich in a dream suggested approaching harm.

The Hebrew governor
The best-remembered story of dream interpretation in ancient Egypt, however, is the biblical tale of Joseph. With God's help he correctly explained several premonitory dreams, notably the pharaoh's vision of seven fat cows

emerging from the Nile only to be swallowed up by the seven lean cows that followed them.

The book of Genesis goes to some lengths to explain how it came about that a foreigner, and a servant at that, came to be consulted by the nation's ruler on so intimate a matter. Joseph was approached, it reveals, on the recommendation of the pharaoh's butler, who had encountered the Hebrew while both were out of favour and in prison. While he was incarcerated, Joseph had correctly interpreted the butler's dream of pressing grapes for the pharaoh as indicating that the man was about to be released.

When the pharaoh heard the butler's story, he decided to test the stranger's skills. Joseph's interpretation of the royal dream – as indicating seven years of plenty to be followed by seven of famine – so impressed the ruler that he rewarded the Hebrew with a ring from his own finger and a golden collar and appointed him Governor of all Egypt. This role gave Joseph responsibility for the contingency planning needed to avert the disaster he had foreseen.

While the story illustrates the importance accorded to premonitory dreams, it also raises questions over the appointment of a foreigner to so high a position in the Egyptian court. This fact has led scholars provisionally to date the events to the Second Intermediate Period. During this time of troubles in the seventeenth and sixteenth centuries BCE, rulers of Semitic stock are known to have held power in Lower Egypt, where Joseph would have been detained.

A Dream Fulfilled

In 1818CE a granite stele was unearthed between the paws of the Great Sphinx at Giza (see right). The inscription describes how Tuthmose IV, who ruled Egypt at the turn of the fourteenth century BCE, once fell asleep in the Sphinx's shadow while out hunting in the desert as a young prince. In his sleep, the Sphinx – covered chin-high with sand at the time – spoke to Tuthmose, predicting that one day he would rule Egypt, even though at the time he had elder brothers with better claims to the succession. In return, the Sphinx asked only to be restored to its former glory, so Tuthmose had workmen clear the sand away from around the creature's body. Some years later the prince did indeed ascend to the throne just as the Sphinx had predicted – whereupon Tuthmose set up the stele as a thanks offering.

aztec visions of the cataclysm

One of the strangest tales in the history of prophecy concerns the demise of Mexico's great Aztec empire. It fell at the hands of the Spanish adventurer Hernán Cortés and his small band of conquistadors in 1519. Although the invaders initially numbered barely 500 men – armed, admittedly, with guns and cannons, which were unknown to the Aztecs – they were able to advance on the Aztec capital of Tenochtitlán (today's Mexico City) virtually unopposed by the imperial forces. On their arrival, they were greeted by the emperor, Motecuhzoma II, in person, and housed in sumptuous quarters near the royal palace. The Spaniards responded to this hospitality by seizing their host and putting him in chains – in due course they conquered his entire empire.

The Plumed Serpent

It was only later that the Spaniards learned the reason for Motecuhzoma's unexpected passivity. Aztec myth told of a benevolent god, Quetzalcoatl, who was represented as the Plumed Serpent (a cross between the brilliantly plumed quetzal bird and a rattlesnake). Over time, this deity became confused with a real-life ruler of the Toltec empire, a precursor of the Aztec realm. This man – a votary of the god Quetzalcoatl – came to be revered as a culture hero who attempted to replace the bloody rites of the region's fierce gods with the gentler cult of his own favoured divinity. However, his reign ended in failure and he left the country, sailing away to the east. But legend, confounding the votary with the god he worshipped, held that he would one day return. When he did so, it would be in the form of a bearded man, whose coming was predicted for the 12th year in one of the 52-year cycles into which the peoples

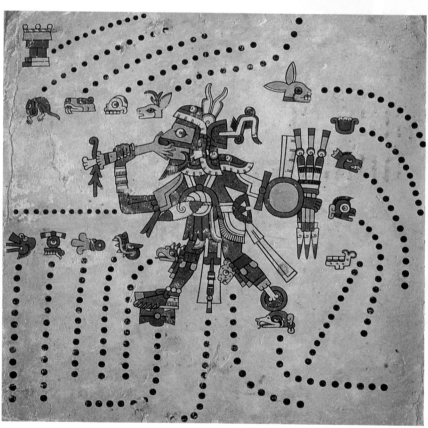

An Aztec codex depiction of the god Tezcatlipoca, whose black divining glass Emperor Motecuhzoma II saw on the head of a huge, grey bird in a dream presaging the arrival of the Spanish invaders.

> "He held it for certain that, as his prophets and soothsayers had predicted, his state and wealth and prosperity would all vanish within a few years through the actions of certain people who would arrive ... to overthrow his good fortune."
>
> (Spanish chronicler Bartolomé de las Casas, of the Aztec emperor Motecuhzoma II)

of Mesoamerica divided their calendar (see pages 94–7).

So, when news of bearded strangers arriving by ship from the east first reached Motecuhzoma's court, it seemed natural to imagine that they might be emissaries sent by Quetzalcoatl. The probability was increased by the fact that 1519, the year of the Spaniards' incursion, was the 12th of the current Aztec cycle. The emperor was also no doubt swayed by reports of the strange, deer-like beasts that the newcomers rode – horses were unknown in Mexico at the time – and of their firearms, which at first hearing must have suggested that the soldiers carried with them the power to produce lightning and thunder.

Omens of doom

Motecuhzoma was an intelligent man, and it seems unlikely that such illusions about the strangers lasted for very long. But the lingering suspicion that the Spaniards might in some way have been sent by Quetzalcoatl does seem to have stayed the king's hand. Accounts of Motecuhzoma's state of mind as the invaders approached his capital suggest he was obsessed with omens of doom. The chroniclers recorded many of these portents, stretching back over almost a decade. Nine years before the Spanish invasion, the lake beside which Tenochtitlán was built had unexpectedly flooded the city, destroying many buildings. Soon after, a raging fire had broken out in one of the turrets of the city's great temple. Subsequently two comets had been seen, and lightning had struck the temple dedicated to Xiuhtecuhtli, god of fire.

Then, shortly before the Spaniards' arrival, Motecuhzoma himself had a dream that seemed to presage disaster. He saw a great grey bird with a black mirror on its forehead – a mirror he recognized as the divining glass of the fearsome god Tezcatlipoca. Peering into the mirror's depths, the king found himself looking at the night sky and its stars, but they soon cleared to reveal an image of oddly-dressed warriors armed with unfamiliar weapons. Alarmed, he asked those of his subjects who had had strange dreams to come forward and repeat them – and then punished those who did so for bearing bad tidings.

When the Spanish finally arrived, their behaviour quickly disabused the king of any illusions he may have had concerning their divine origin. By then, however, it was too late to take effective action against the invaders. For Motecuhzoma, crippled by forebodings of impending disaster, forewarned had, in his case, meant disarmed.

A warning from beyond the grave

One of the stranger legends about the Spanish conquest of Mexico is probably best interpreted as a dream premonition. It describes how Papantzin, one of Motecuhzoma II's sisters, appeared to the Aztec emperor four days after her own burial. In the dream, she warned her brother of the approach of ships bearing helmeted men who posed a serious threat to his empire. After the Conquest, reports of the story reached the Spanish chroniclers, who vouched for the integrity of their sources, even to the extent of sending legally drawn-up attestations of the story's truth to the Vatican.

premonitions of death

The American president Abraham Lincoln was very disturbed by a dream in which he foresaw his own death. This painting, from a private collection, depicts the moment when Lincoln questions an attendant soldier and discovers that the dead man lying in state is in fact himself.

On the evening of 11 April 1865, Abraham Lincoln was entertaining guests at the White House. In spite of the fact that Robert E. Lee had capitulated at Appomattox Court House just two days earlier, and the Civil War was virtually won at last, the American president was in sombre mood. The talk turned to dreams, and Lincoln commented on how often they featured in scripture. "If we believe the Bible," he said, "we must accept the

> ## "'who is dead in the white House?' I demanded of one of the soldiers. 'The president,' was his answer, 'he was killed by an assassin.'"
>
> (ABRAHAM LINCOLN, THREE DAYS BEFORE
> HIS ASSASSINATION, AS RECORDED BY
> COL. WARD H. LAMON, A WHITE HOUSE AIDE)

fact that, in the old days, God and his angels came to men in their sleep and made themselves known in dreams." Then he went on to recount a dream of his own that had been troubling him for several days.

In the dream, Lincoln saw himself wandering from room to room in the White House. A deathlike stillness hung over the place, broken by the subdued sound of sobbing. Lincoln eventually ended up in the East Room, where he saw a corpse lying on a catafalque, guarded by soldiers and surrounded by mourners. He asked one of the bystanders who it was that was dead, and was told that it was the president, killed by an assassin. At that point, just as a terrible outburst of grief swept the crowd, Lincoln woke up.

"I slept no more that night," he told his guests, "and although it was only a dream I have been strangely annoyed by it ever since." Three days later, Lincoln was shot by John Wilkes Booth as he watched a play at Ford's Theatre in Washington DC. The president died at 7.22 the following morning.

Foreseeing one's own demise

There are, of course, rational arguments that go some way to explaining such phenomena. Lincoln, for instance, evidently knew he was hated by supporters of the defeated South, and had good reason to fear assassination. Even so, some stories defy easy explanation. One example concerns Robert Morris, an eighteenth-century tobacco planter whose better-known son of the same name was the banker remembered as "the financier of the American Revolution". Morris tried to call off the ceremonial inspection of a warship after dreaming that he would be killed by the discharge of one of its cannons. He eventually let himself be persuaded to go ahead with the visit, but only after the captain of the vessel promised that no guns would be fired until Morris was safely back on shore. Morris's party duly toured the ship, and were being rowed back to land when the captain inadvertently raised his hand to brush away a fly. Mistaking the gesture for a signal to fire the salute, a gunner discharged his cannon and Morris was killed by shrapnel from the shot, just as he had foreseen.

An even earlier case involves a member of the illustrious Italian Sforza family who, in 1523, dreamed that he would meet his death by drowning. Passing near the castle of Pescara next day, he saw a child fall into a river and waded into the water to try to save her. However, the weight of the armour he was wearing pulled him down into the mud, and he duly drowned.

A messenger of death

Another well-publicized case of a death that was dreamed about in advance took place in eighteenth-century London. On 24 November 1779, Thomas Lord Lyttelton, a 35-year-old nobleman, was disturbed in his sleep just after midnight by a sound that he described as resembling a bird fluttering among the curtains of his four-poster bed. He then saw a vision of a woman in white who pointed her finger at him accusingly and told him that he would be dead within three days.

Word of the apparition quickly spread around the city's coffee houses, and the young lord's predicted death became a popular talking point. Lyttelton himself retired to his country estate near Epsom in Surrey to wait out the three days. As the hours ticked away on 27 November, his mood lightened considerably, for he felt in good health. Lyttelton went to his room at 11 o'clock that evening, convinced that he had nothing to fear. His manservant helped him to undress, and then left the room briefly on an errand. He returned a few minutes later to find his master having a fit. The attack proved

across the species barrier

In 1904 the 48-year-old English novelist Henry Rider Haggard, author of *King Solomon's Mines*, reported having a premonition of the death of an animal – his daughter's black retriever. He dreamed that he saw the dog lying among brushwood by water where, he later recorded, the animal "transmitted to my mind in an undefined fashion the knowledge that it was dying". Waking, he described the dream to his wife. The couple subsequently discovered that the dog was indeed missing. Its body was eventually found caught against a weir in a local river, not far from the family home. Haggard concluded that the pet had succeeded in communicating with him by "placing whatever portion of my being is capable of receiving such impulses when enchained by sleep into its own terrible position".

fatal – before the clock had struck midnight Lord Lyttelton was dead. The premonition had proved correct.

Intimations of death do not always come in dream form. Other celebrities who had some inkling of their own demise include the well-known American writer Mark Twain. He told a friend that, having been born in a year when Halley's comet passed close to the Earth, he expected to pass away at the time of its next visit. Sure enough, Twain died the day after the comet's return appearance, 75 years later, on 20 April 1910.

The composer Arnold Schoenberg was superstitious about numbers and particularly feared the number 13. He became convinced that he would die in his 76th year, because the digits add together to make 13. When, in late 1950, he reached the age of 76, Schoenberg awaited the arrival of the 13th day of each month with apprehension. In

July 1951, when the 13th fell on a Friday, he decided to keep to his bed. However, even this precaution was not enough save him. He passed away at precisely 13 minutes to midnight, and the last word he uttered was "Harmony!"

Foretelling another's death

Of course, a person's expectation of his or her own death may to some extent prove self-fulfilling – the stress generated by the fear of dying could itself conceivably bring on a fatal attack. The advance awareness of another individual's death is in some ways harder to explain. Yet stories of such premonitions are found in every culture.

A classic example of this type of foresight is contained in Nathaniel Wanley's *The Wonders of the Little World*, which is a curious work published in 1788. The book recounts the experience of an English gentleman living in Prague

who woke up one morning in the certainty that, at home in England, his father was dead. He was so shaken by the vividness of the dream that he wrote down the time and circumstances in a notebook, which was later packed in a chest along with his other possessions and sent back to England.

It was four years before the gentleman himself returned home, during which time he received confirmation that his father had indeed died. On his return to England, the gentleman assembled his sisters and certain friends of the family to attend the opening of the chest. The witnesses were then able to confirm that the date on which he had written his account of the dream had in fact been the very day of his father's demise.

According to Wanley, the same individual claimed also to have shared a premonition with his brother at the time of his mother's death many years before. When they were students, both young men had, on the same night, dreamed of hearing their mother regretting that she would not be able to go to Cambridge to see her son receive his master's degree. If the story can be believed, it suggests that a "premonition" may exist independently, to be received by more than one person.

Life-saving visions

Sometimes premonitions can play a direct part in saving lives. Anecdotes about individuals who have escaped death in disaster situations as a result of dreams or intuitions are well known. Here too, history provides some curious examples, including one involving Francesco Petrarca, the Italian Renaissance poet. Knowing that a friend of his was ill, Petrarca dreamed that the invalid appeared before him with a message: he would shortly receive a visit from someone whose help the sick man badly needed. Soon after the poet woke up, there was a knock at his door. The visitor turned out to be his friend's physician, who had come to warn Petrarca that his patient was on the point of death. Encouraged by his dream, Petrarca begged the doctor not to give up hope and to go back to the sick bed. After further ministrations, the dying man revived and in time was restored to health.

A story from the First World War suggests that wider events than one individual's death might hang on dreams. It tells of a 28-year-old German corporal serving on the Somme who was having trouble sleeping in the dugout he shared with a dozen companions. Waking up from a nightmare in which he felt himself crushed under tons of earth, it occurred to him that the dream might have been intended as a warning, even though at the time there was a lull in the artillery bombardments that regularly swept the trenches. Taking no chances, the corporal made his way outside to get some fresh air.

He had only been outside for a short time when he heard the whistle of an approaching shell. He turned around to find that the projectile had scored a direct hit on the dugout. Most of his companions were killed instantly by the blast, and no doubt he would have been too if he had not acted on his fears. In that case history itself might have been changed, for the young soldier in question was Adolf Hitler.

Lord Lyttelton's dream in which a woman in white appeared to warn him of his impending death is captured in this coloured engraving from The Astrologer, *1825. Samuel Johnson, the lexicographer, called the event the most extraordinary thing to have happened in his time.*

Dreams that foretold Disasters

The 1941 Japanese attack on the US naval base at Pearl Harbor, pictured here, cost more than 2,000 lives and brought the United States into the Second World War. The surprise attack may have been foreseen by an anonymous individual in Owensville, Indiana, two years before the event.

Graffiti is an age-old phenomenon, and so the appearance of the words "REMEMBER PEARL HARBOR", painted on the sidewalk in front of the entrance to the primary school in Owensville, Indiana, might not in itself seem remarkable. However, what is striking in the story is the date when the message was written: 7 December 1939, two years to the day before the Japanese attack on the US naval station in Hawaii.

Unless some local individual had private reasons for commemorating the naval base, or people's subsequent memories of the event were simply wrong, the precocious appearance of the message would seem to suggest a case of precognition. If so, the example is far from unique. People have been reporting advance glimpses of disaster since classical times and even earlier. The phenomenon is closely allied to premonitions of death, but operates on a wider scale, embracing wars, crimes of violence and natural catastrophes as well as the fate of individuals.

A prophet of doom

One early example of a seer whose predictions proved correct comes from the Romano-Jewish historian Josephus's account of the Jewish War. He reports that a certain Jesus, son of Ananias, started to prophesy tragedy for Jerusalem four years before the revolt of 66CE that ended in the destruction of the Temple by Roman legionaries and, eventually, in the Jewish diaspora itself (see page 15). Jesus, son of Ananias, was arrested and tortured for his pains, but continued to call down woe on the city both before and after the outbreak of fighting, right up to the time of the siege of Jerusalem itself. Then, as the tragedy he had long foreseen was happening all around him, he was finally silenced when, in the course of the battle, a stone fell on his head and killed him.

Murder foreseen

Perhaps because of their abruptness and dramatic quality, political assassinations seem to be a focus for precognitive dreams and visions. The most publicized

prediction of this kind in recent times concerned the shooting of US president John F. Kennedy in Dallas in November 1963. The prediction was made by Jeanne Dixon, an American clairvoyant who had become a celebrity as a result of her syndicated newspaper columns and television appearances. In her authorized biography, written within a couple of years of Kennedy's death, Mrs Dixon claimed to have had repeated premonitions of the tragedy. These began 11 years before the event and climaxed on the fatal day itself, when she reportedly told two society ladies with whom she was lunching that something dreadful was about to happen. Specifically, she cited an interview that she had given to *Parade* magazine in 1956, in which she claimed to have predicted that "a blue-eyed Democratic president elected in 1960" would be assassinated.

misleading Dreams

Alongside the accurate previsions, history has several examples of premonitory dreams that proved to be disastrously wrong. The Roman historian Valerius Maximus recorded that Hannibal was encouraged to lead the troops of his native Carthage to invade Italy in 219BCE by an angelic figure that appeared to him in his sleep. "Go!" the apparition told him, "the fates are there to be accomplished." Hannibal went, but despite a brilliant campaign, failed to crush Rome. He ended up taking poison to avoid the humiliation of defeat and capture.

Similarly, the fifth-century-BCE Persian emperor Xerxes was impelled by a figure that appeared to him in a dream to invade Greece against the advice of his generals. According to Herodotus, the apparition came to Xerxes twice and then to his advisor Artabanus, bearing the same message. Yet the emperor's forces suffered disastrous defeats at the battles of Salamis (see page 26) and Plataea and were driven out of Greece, bringing to an end Persian dreams of conquering the country.

This 19th-century oil painting depicts the Persian emperor Xerxes I about to cross the Hellespont on his way to invade Greece in 480BCE.

In fact the report as published was rather less specific, stating: "As for the 1960 election, Mrs Dixon thinks it will be dominated by Labor and won by a Democrat. But he will be assassinated or die in office, though not necessarily in his first term." The accuracy of the prediction is still striking, though perhaps it becomes a little less so in the light of the well-publicized chain of coincidence that had seen every US president elected in a year ending in "0" since Lincoln's day die in office. Besides Kennedy himself, Lincoln (1860), Garfield (1880) and McKinley (1900) were all shot; Warren Harding (1920) and F.D. Roosevelt (1940) both died in office. The chain was finally broken by Ronald Reagan (1980), who survived an assassination attempt in 1981 and went on to see out two full terms in the White House.

In some ways the story of John Williams, a mining engineer from Redruth in Cornwall, southwest England, makes a more convincing case for prevision. On the night of 11 May 1812 he dreamed that he was in the House of Commons at Westminster in the presence of a small man in a blue coat and white waistcoat. As Williams watched, a man in a brown coat with yellow buttons drew a pistol and shot the smaller man. The gunman was then apprehended, and Williams recollected being told that the man he had fired at was "the chancellor". Waking, he recounted the dream to his wife, then went back to sleep, only to see the same scene twice more. The next day he told the story to everyone he encountered.

It was only later in the day that Williams met his son, fresh from Truro with news that had just arrived with the mail coach from London. There had been an assassination in the House of Commons the previous evening. The victim was Spencer Perceval, Britain's prime minister and chancellor of the exchequer (finance minister), who had been shot dead by a bankrupt Liverpool broker, John Bellingham. Even though he knew neither of the two men by sight, Williams's dream description of the pair and their clothes matched the events perfectly. On a subsequent visit to London, Williams was also able to identify the spot where the killing took place without being told.

Premonitions of catastrophe

As subjects for premonitory dreams, air-, land- and sea-travel disasters are probably as common as political assassinations. There is plenty of anecdotal evidence of people whose lives have been saved because a sixth sense prevented them from boarding a train, boat or plane that subsequently crashed. If some intriguing research undertaken by one American mathematician in the 1960s holds true generally, the number may even run into many thousands. William Cox examined the numbers of passengers travelling on trains that had crashed and then compared the figures with the passenger load on the same trains on normal days. He found significantly fewer people on board on the days when the accidents happened. For example, a Chicago and Illinois train known as the "Georgian" crashed on 15 June 1952 with just nine passengers aboard; the average number of passengers for the same train over the four preceding weeks had been nearly 50. Even though many factors, such as weather conditions, may have affected passenger volume, Cox believed that the figures showed the existence of an "accident avoidance" phenomenon based on subconscious premonitions.

The notion of isolated, individual previsions of disasters, often at a distance, is more widely accepted. One well-known case involved a 23-year-old Cincinatti man, David Booth, who for 10 days in a row dreamed of a plane crash involving an American Airlines flight. Convinced that his nightmare was premonitory, Booth

"It wasn't like a dream. It was like I was standing there watching the whole thing – like watching television."

(David Booth, foreteller of the American Airlines DC-10 crash, quoted in *Predictions* by Joe Fisher)

The mass burial of some of the victims of the Aberfan slag-heap avalanche of 1966. Several dozen people claimed to have had a premonition of the tragedy.

insights like David Booth's, but all have foundered due to the lack of specific data in the warnings received. Without exact details of locations and times, even sympathetically-minded authorities can hardly be expected to take action on dreamed warnings, however compelling.

One catastrophe that was well investigated after the event was the tragedy that struck a Welsh mining community shortly after 9 am on the morning of 21 October 1966. After two days of heavy rain, coal waste piled on a slag heap outside Aberfan suddenly slipped down a hillside on the edge of the village, engulfing a primary school, a row of terraced houses and a farm. In all, 28 adults and 116 children were buried alive.

In the wake of the avalanche, a London psychiatrist appealed for accounts of premonitions of the disaster. He received 76 replies, 60 of which he considered worthy of investigation. After taking more detailed statements and seeking corroborative testimonies, he was prepared to lend credence to 24 of the premonitions on the grounds that they had been divulged to third parties before the tragedy happened. Almost all of these visions had occurred in dreams. One elderly man had seen the word "Aberfan" spelled out in bright lights; a woman in Kent saw a momentary apparition of a school building engulfed in an avalanche of coal; a spiritualist from Devon claimed to have seen a terrified small boy standing by a rescue worker with a peaked cap – a pair she recognized after the event in television coverage of the relief effort.

The saddest story of all came from the mother of one of the dead children. Her nine-year-old daughter had woken from a dream two weeks before the disaster to announce that she was not afraid to die because she knew she would be with her friends. Then, on the eve of the tragedy, the child reported a second dream – this time she had seen the school covered in blackness. The girl died in the school that morning; with her were the friends whose names she had earlier mentioned.

immediately contacted both the airline itself and the Federal Aviation Authority to warn them of impending danger, but sadly he could give no details of the time or location of the accident in his vision. In fact it came three days after his calls, on 25 May 1979, at Chicago's O'Hare airport. An American Airlines DC-10 crashed on take-off, killing 273 people – the worst air disaster to that date in American history.

Several attempts have been made to set up premonitions bureaux that could take advantage of

The sinking of the *Titanic*

The New York Times.

TITANIC SINKS FOUR HOURS AFTER HITTING ICEBERG; 866 RESCUED BY CARPATHIA, PROBABLY 1250 PERISH; ISMAY SAFE, MRS. ASTOR MAYBE, NOTED NAMES MISSING

The Lost Titanic Being Towed Out of Belfast Harbor.

CAPT. E. J. SMITH.

The New York Times *reports the loss of the* Titanic *on 15 April 1912. It was later confirmed that more than 1,500 people had died.*

No single disaster has attracted greater attention among investigators of the paranormal than the sinking of the *Titanic* on the night of 14–15 April 1912. The size and sumptuous luxury of the vessel, its reputation for unsinkability, and the drama of its disappearance in the freezing North Atlantic night have all helped to etch its final moments indelibly in the popular imagination.

Entire books have been written about the premonitions experienced by passengers on the *Titanic*, and by others who refused to board it because of some sixth sense of impending doom. One American businessman cancelled his reservation for the fateful journey after receiving a letter and a cable from his wife in Nebraska – she had dreamed that she saw the *Titanic* go down. A woman watching the ship setting out from port through the Solent suddenly declared, "That ship is going to sink before it reaches America!" and angrily urged those around her to do something to stop the vessel.

The prophetic writer

Yet the most intriguing preview of the fate of the liner appeared long before the *Titanic* was even conceived, let alone built or launched. It came from the pen of a little-known American novelist and short-story writer named Morgan Robertson. A sailor in his youth, Robertson later turned to writing to earn a living, looking to his maritime past to provide the background for his short stories. Robertson never found writing easy, and would sit for hours waiting for inspiration. Then, when the mood came on him, he would write feverishly. In the words of one of his friends, he "implicitly believed that some discarnate soul, some spirit entity with literary ability, denied physical expression, had commandeered his body and brain". Robertson liked to call this demon of inspiration his "astral writing partner".

In 1898, 14 years before the *Titanic* sank, Robertson felt impelled to undertake a novella. Entitled *Futility*, it turned out to be extraordinarily prophetic. It was set on a luxurious British liner sailing across the North Atlantic. The ship – the biggest of its time – was said to be unsinkable. In the novel the vessel sets out on its maiden voyage in April, and then smashes into an iceberg and goes down with the loss of many hundreds of lives. The number of the dead is increased because of an inadequate provision of lifeboats. In all these details Robertson accurately predicted the fate of the *Titanic*. However, the most remarkable coincidence of all lay in the name he chose to give his ship – the *Titan*.

A contemporary watercolour depicts the Titanic going down after hitting an iceberg. Stories of individuals who experienced premonitions of the tragedy abound. The author of at least one book has set out to refute such claims, seeking logical explanations for them all. Yet the sheer number of supposed premonitions is itself impressive.

In other details too Robertson came remarkably close to the reality of 1912. He gave his vessel 3 propellors, 19 watertight compartments and 24 lifeboats; the corresponding figures for the *Titanic* were 3, 16 and 20. The *Titan* had 3,000 people aboard, and struck the iceberg at a speed of 25 knots; the *Titanic* carried a company of 2,224 and was travelling at 23 knots at the fateful moment. Critics have pointed out that, as a man of the sea, Robertson could have been expected to have a reasonably clear idea of what the specifications of a future luxury liner might be, and how it could be expected to perform. Yet even so, whether his work is best categorized under the heading of premonition or of rational prediction, it remains one of history's most extraordinary examples of accurate prevision.

A warning unheeded

More than two decades before he went to his death with the *Titanic*, the well-known English journalist and spiritualist W.T. Stead published a story entitled "How the Mail Steamer Went Down in Mid-Atlantic, by a Survivor". In the story a giant ocean liner sinks following a collision with another ship. Due to a shortage of lifeboats on the liner, there is a great loss of life. Stead wrote: "This is exactly what might take place, and what will take place, if liners are sent to sea short of boats". Tragically, he was later proved right — there were only enough lifeboats on board the *Titanic* to accommodate half its passengers.

an experiment with time

The eruption of Mount Pelée, on the island of Martinique in May 1902 is portrayed in this contemporary illustration. Two accounts of dream premonitions of the tragedy have been recorded – one experienced by J.W. Dunne and one by Ferdinand Clere (see box, page 70).

In 1899 a 24-year-old aeronautical engineer named John William Dunne had the first of a series of dreams which, in time, would change his life. In itself, what he dreamed that night was unexceptional enough – even trivial. Dunne saw himself arguing with a waiter in a hotel. The subject of the dispute was the time of day – both agreed that it was 4.30, but Dunne thought that it was the afternoon while the waiter insisted it was the middle of the

night. Dunne subsequently woke up and checked his watch, only to find that it had stopped at the moment of his waking, precisely at 4.30 am.

Many people would have thought no more of the incident, but Dunne liked to fathom out problems (some years later he would design Britain's first military aircraft). He was fascinated by the fact that he had known the time in his dream without having looked at the watch. It seemed to be a case of clairvoyance.

Premonitions and headlines

In 1901 Dunne found himself on the Italian Riviera, recuperating from an injury received while fighting in the Boer War. He dreamed that he was in a small town in the Sudan, where he saw three ragged, deeply tanned explorers approaching from the south. He questioned them and was told that they had "come right through from the Cape". The next morning, his newspaper contained an item headlined: "The Cape-to-

Cairo *Daily Telegraph* Expedition at Khartoum". The article described the arrival of a three-man team in the Sudanese capital in the course of a journey up the length of Africa.

Dunne's next significant dream was particularly dramatic. He saw himself on a mountainside where jets of steam were escaping from fissures in the ground. Intuitively, he realized that he was on an island dominated by a volcano that was about to blow up. His one aim then became to save the inhabitants, and the rest of the dream was spent in increasingly frantic attempts to persuade the authorities (who turned out to be French) to organize an evacuation. Dunne remembered repeating to everyone he met that 4,000 people would die unless something was done.

The significance of the dream became clear from another newspaper headline a few days later: "Volcano Disaster in Martinique. Town Swept Away. An Avalanche of Flame. Probable Loss of 40,000 Lives". The eruption of Mount Pelée on the French Caribbean island was the most disastrous of the twentieth century in terms of lives lost. One detail that Dunne subsequently noted was that his 4,000 was actually 40,000 in the report; he was out by a zero. However, he only noticed the discrepancy several years later when he was researching the incident; at the time he read the figure as "4,000", a fact that persuaded him that his premonition was actually of reading the newspaper account rather than of viewing the tragedy itself.

Other dreams followed. In one, Dunne saw himself on a wooden structure with a fire hose playing upon it, surrounded by people and covered in smoke. This time the newspaper reported a fire at a rubber factory outside Paris. The fumes had been so dense that many employees had died from smoke inhalation, even on the outside balcony where they had gone to await rescue. There were more personal visions, too: of a mad horse charging down a path on which Dunne was walking, and of an aeroplane accident involving an acquaintance of Dunne's. Both events actually happened the day after Dunne dreamed them, although with significant differences from the dream version. In the first case the horse was smaller and the setting slightly different, while in the second Dunne's acquaintance – a passenger in the plane – was killed; in the dream he had been flying the craft and had survived.

The final dream that Dunne chose to relate was a classic disaster premonition. He saw a train crash at a location he recognized as lying just north of the Firth of Forth on Scotland's east coast; several carriages were lying on the side of an embankment and on flat grassland below. While still half-asleep, Dunne was conscious enough of the significance of the image to strive to ascertain a date, and understood that it was sometime in the following spring (he had the dream in the autumn of 1913). Sure enough, on 14 April 1914 the express mail train between London and Edinburgh, one of the most famous mail trains of the day, left the rails about 12 miles (20 km) north of the Forth Bridge and rolled onto a golf course below.

Time travel

The obvious inference to draw from this remarkable sequence of previsions was that Dunne had exceptional psychic gifts. However, he himself rejected that conclusion.

"was it possible ... that dreams — dreams in general, all dreams, everybody's dreams — were composed of images of past experience and images of future experience blended together in approximately equal proportions?"

(J.W. DUNNE, *AN EXPERIMENT WITH TIME*)

A family saved

J.W. Dunne was not the only man to have a prophetic dream about the eruption of Mount Pelée in 1902. On Martinique itself, Ferdinand Clere, a sugar planter who lived in St Pierre, near the foot of the volcano, was woken by a nightmare in which the mountain exploded. At first he took no action, but when word came of an initial spasm that had sent a flow of lava down over a sugar factory, Clere at once decided, on the evidence of his dream, that there was worse to come. Gathering together his family and valuables, he fled the town, much to the amusement of some neighbours, who thought that he was overreacting. Three days later the entire town, the ruins of which are visible in the photograph above, was engulfed by the outflow from a second, more massive discharge. All but a single inhabitant were killed.

In demeanour and upbringing he was an Edwardian gentleman – the writer J.B. Priestley, an admirer, said that Dunne "looked and behaved like the old regular officer type crossed with a mathematician and engineer". To such a man, unconventionality of any sort was not a desirable trait. Dunne wrote: "No-one, I imagine, can derive any considerable pleasure from the supposition that he is a freak".

So, instead, Dunne came up with a remarkable proposition. He claimed that everyone has the ability to move backward and forward through time in their dreams. He suggested that dreams are made up of fragmentary impressions of past and future events in roughly equal proportions. Dunne maintained that most people are unaware of this capacity only because very few bother to remember exactly what they have dreamed. Were they to do so, he insisted, they would soon start to notice details manifesting themselves in the hours and days ahead.

Dunne spelled out his ideas in a book called *An Experiment with Time*, which was published in 1927 and attracted considerable attention. Priestley hailed it as "one of the most fascinating, the most curious, and perhaps the most important books of this age", and it helped inspire his so-called "time plays" – *Time and the Conways* and *An Inspector Calls*.

Recording dreams

The most immediate effect the book had was to promote a fashion for

A foreglimpse of the gallows

In elaborating his theories, Dunne accepted that some exceptional premonitions could long predate their fulfilment. In one eighteenth-century case, the interval was more than six years. The dreamer was a certain Mr Cunningham, a friend of the English poet Anna Seward. While waiting once with a friend to meet her, Cunningham described two vivid scenes he had witnessed as he slept the previous night. One was of a rider being stopped and searched by three men, and then apprehended; in the other he saw the same man hanging on a gallows. Soon after Seward arrived, bringing with her a stranger whom she introduced as John André, a newly commissioned British officer soon off to join his regiment in Canada. Cunningham recognized him at once as the horseman he had seen in his dream. André hardly seemed like gallows material, but events were to prove Cunningham's vision prophetic. Serving as a major on the British side in the American War of Independence, André conspired with Benedict Arnold to seize the fortress of West Point. He was arrested, searched for incriminating documents, and then hanged as a spy, just as the dream had indicated.

keeping dream diaries. Dunne himself believed that writing down dreams straight after waking was the only way to "fix" the details so that they could subsequently be checked against reality. He set strict rules for their reporting. The best time to expect premonitory dreams, he maintained, was before days when unfamiliar things might happen, so he suggested selecting the nights before journeys or similar special events. He stressed the importance of taking notes immediately on waking, and observed that a short record full of details – particularly any that might seem unusual in daily life – was more useful than a longer, vaguer account. He also insisted that the account should separate the actual images seen from the interpretation put upon them, on the grounds that the dreaming mind often misread what it was seeing. As an example he cited a real-life experience of sparks from a fire blowing into his face, which he had taken in his dream for a crowd of people throwing lighted cigarette butts at him.

Dunne proposed reading over the entire dream diary at the end of every day of the experiment. He suggested a two-day limit for matching small details to subsequent events, while allowing that the interval could be "extended in ratio to the oddity and unusualness of the incident". His own dream of the railway accident in Scotland predated the actual crash by roughly six months. Finally, there was the question of marking the dreams. His own system was to indicate with a simple cross those that, in his view, had decisively evoked a single incident. Dreams that contained a partial revelation of something that later happened – some significant detail rather than the whole story – were noted with a cross enclosed in a circle.

Dunne himself tried out his system on seven volunteers, including himself. He recorded a total of 88 dreams in all, in which he claimed to have traced 14 resemblances to the past, five of them good and the rest mostly moderate, and 20 reflections of future events, five good, six moderate and nine indifferent. Yet, as the writer Geoffrey Ashe has pointed out, Dunne's findings tended to undermine his own theory, for 15 of the 20 "future" hits were in fact recorded by just two of the seven dreamers, Dunne himself being one of them.

In retrospect, Dunne's work remains remarkable as one of the few serious attempts to come to terms with the problems posed by premonitory dreams, although few people now would accept the complex theory of "serialism" (viewing time as an infinite sequence of overlapping layers) that he based on his experiences. If anything, Dunne himself becomes more interesting for the prescience he undoubtedly displayed. Despite his gentlemanly reticence, it is hard not to conclude that he did have uncommon gifts denied to most other people.

systems of divination

If the shamanistic tradition of inspired prophecy harks back deep into the hunter-gatherer past, a parallel vein of formalized divination can be traced at least to the first organized societies. Sumer, Babylon and Egypt all had their professional diviners. Where the prophets relied on an inner voice to guide them, the soothsayers made use of structured frameworks that provided them with fixed methods for foretelling what was to come. Sometimes such systems claimed to have science on their side: classical astrology and the calendrical systems of the Aztecs and Maya, for example, both drew on formidable mathematical skills and what was, for their day, an advanced knowledge of the heavens. Other institutions, such as Roman augury or druid omen-watching, sought to tease out the will of the gods from the transient phenomena of nature. In China the *Yi Jing* drew on local traditions of synchronicity and the notion that everything that happens at a given moment is somehow interconnected. However, the purest system of all was the art of scrying. By gazing into their mirrors or crystal balls, scryers sought to glimpse the future in their own minds, untroubled by any considerations but the projection of their subconscious intuitions.

The ancient roots of astrology

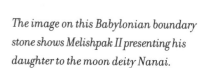

In its day, astrology was the most intellectually satisfying of all predictive systems. It proposed a holistic vision of the universe with the Earth at its centre. An awesome celestial clockwork kept the stars and planets in their courses, eternally circling the human world on reliable, predestined paths. By intense mental application, the astrologer could work out mathematically the pattern of the whole, projecting forward not just the movements of the stars but the compelling influence they must exert on the sublunary world below.

The roots of astrology can be traced back to Babylon, where sky-gazing first took on the attributes of a serious science. From early on, a connection was made between events on Earth and in the heavens, and priests scanned the sky for omens. A collection of more than 7,000 observations, known as the *Enuma Anu Enlil*, has survived on cuneiform tablets excavated from the library of the Assyrian king Ashurbanipal at Nineveh. They show that such signs as lunar halos, eclipses and the first appearances of the planets were monitored. These were seen as signalling good or evil fortune for the state, and particularly for the royal family, who seem to have been the diviners' principal patrons.

The image on this Babylonian boundary stone shows Melishpak II presenting his daughter to the moon deity Nanai.

The reputation of the Babylonian star-gazers spread far and wide in the ancient Middle East. They were the "Chaldeans" of the Old Testament (see page 13), whose name became synonymous with reading the future in the stars. It was they who first tracked the course of the ecliptic — the path the sun follows against the fixed stars in the course of a year, as observed from Earth. This discovery was to be the base on which horoscopy was founded.

Seers of the zodiac

The birth of astrology proper appears to have followed Alexander the Great's conquest of Mesopotamia in 330BCE and the meeting of Babylonian and classical Greek culture that ensued. A new centre of learning developed at Alexandria, the city that Alexander founded on Egypt's Mediterranean coast. Here, following the duodecimal pattern already established for the months, Greek-speaking savants divided the ecliptic into 12 equidistant sections, each covering 30° of the sun's 360°

> "The place of venus means wherever he may go it will be favourable; he will have sons and daughters .... The place of mercury means the brave one will be first in rank; he will be more important than his brothers."
>
> (READING INSCRIBED ON A CLAY TABLET FOR A CHILD IN SYRIA CA. 200BCE, SAID TO BE THE EARLIEST EXTANT HOROSCOPE)

journey. Each section was associated with the pattern of stars visible in the relevant portion of the night sky, for in the astronomy of the time the Earth was considered the centre of the universe, with the sun and moon orbiting around it against a backdrop of fixed stars. The 12 constellations thus observed eventually became known as the signs of the zodiac.

The 12 "houses" into which the ecliptic was divided provided the background for astrology – the chessboard on which the game of fate was played out. The pieces themselves were the planets. These were not fixed but peripatetic, and their wanderings were thought to exert a powerful influence. The classical world knew only five planets,

and at some early stage each one was assigned certain characteristics; astrologers would claim that the attribution was empirical, based on the knowledge gained from long experience of horoscopy. Mars was linked with assertiveness and aggression, Venus with beauty and love, Jupiter with optimism and justice, Saturn with caution and practicality and Mercury with speed and messages. The constellations likewise mysteriously acquired personalities of their own – Leo grand and overbearing, Gemini rapid and versatile, and so on. By the combination of the two, complicated and refined through an almost endless sophistication of division and subdivision, astrology was born.

At the time, astrology was almost the perfect science, linking each aspect of life on Earth with the machine-like working of the rest of the universe. In its extreme form astrology was completely deterministic: the seer who, by close study of his charts, could compute all the movements of the heavenly bodies could, in theory at least, work out the pattern of the past and the future. In practice, most astrologers made less extreme claims; they

Built ca. 2100BCE, the ziggurat at Ur, 140 miles (225 km) south of Babylon, was one of the great Sumerian temples of ancient Mesopotamia. The ziggurat had seven levels, representing the seven planes of existence and the seven heavenly bodies.

maintained that the planets exerted an influence on people's lives, but still allowed individuals a degree of free will to move with or against the pull of the heavens.

The new science spread rapidly east, reaching India by at least the second century CE and then moving on with Buddhist missionaries to China (where a separate but allied tradition developed) and southeast Asia. Astrology also became firmly entrenched in Iran, and later in the Islamic countries and the Byzantine lands of eastern Europe and the Near East. Oddly, almost the only region where astrology remained virtually unknown was western Europe in the centuries following the collapse of the Roman empire; knowledge of astrology was lost with knowledge of Greek, in which most of its key texts were written. It was only in the twelfth and thirteenth centuries, with the first stirrings of the Renaissance, that the science was rediscovered, largely thanks to translations of Arabic treatises made under Moorish influence in Spain.

Thereafter astrologers flourished in all the European countries. Astrologers were routinely consulted by rulers and politicians, and their discipline held a prestigious position in the universities spreading across the continent. Astrology seemed not just an intellectually valid science but also a centrally important one.

Decline and revival

All that changed with the scientific revolution of the sixteenth and seventeenth centuries. When the new science displaced the Earth from its position at the centre of the universe, the old astrological beliefs were almost literally blown out of the sky. The collapse of the astrologers' reputation took well over a century from the time of Copernicus's discoveries. When the truth finally sank in, the effect was shattering: astrology lost all credibility as a science, for the entire groundwork of astronomical belief on which it had been built was gone.

In the first place, the ecliptic, which had seemed to be the highway along which the sun revolved about

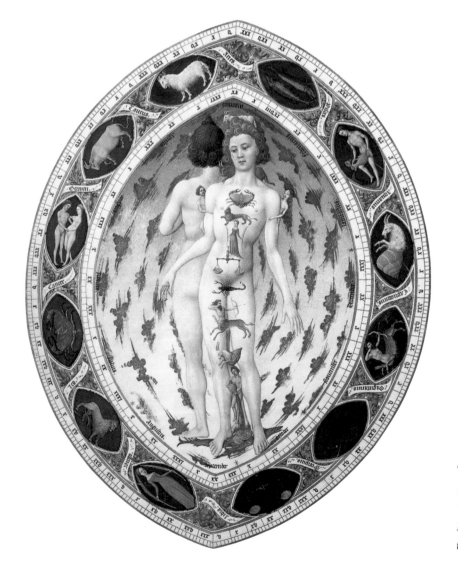

The Anatomy of Man *from the early 15th-century French manuscript entitled "Les Très Riches Heures du Duc de Berry". In the picture's border are the symbols of the 12 signs of the zodiac.*

> "all that has taken place in the past, all that will happen in the future — everything is revealed to [the astrologer], since he knows the effects of the heavenly motions that have been, those that are, and those that will be."
>
> (The thirteenth-century Italian astrologer Guido Bonatti, claiming omniscience for his science)

the Earth, turned out to have no objective existence at all – its only reality lay in human perceptions of the annual solar round. It was not even constant; the phenomenon known as the precession of the equinoxes, caused by the Earth's wobbling motion as it spins through space, meant that it was steadily shifting, at a sufficiently noticeable pace for the zodiac to have moved by one entire house since the initial schema was elaborated. Then again, the constellations themselves were not patterns of light indelibly printed on the firmament's outer sphere. They too were in the eye of the beholder, being composed of individual stars often many thousands of light years apart and lying at hugely differing distances from the Earth.

Astrology has never recovered from the blow dealt to it by the scientific advances made by Copernicus, Galileo and Newton. Its rout at the hands of astronomy makes its revived popularity in the

twentieth century all the more surprising, for horoscopy is now bigger business than at any time in the past, having found a new home in the mass media. Equally hard to explain in logical terms are the undoubted successes scored today as in the past by some individual astrologers. Sceptics must now put

these successes down to a certain innate or acquired predictive talent on the part of the individual forecaster, rather than to the influence of the stars.

The continued demand for horoscopes proves that astrology fulfils a real human need. And, curiously enough, science has now turned up a new predictive discipline of its own. This is the study of genetics and heredity, currently reckoned to account for as much as two-thirds of each individual's personality traits and abilities. It is not too risky a prophecy to suggest that human ingenuity will in time invent a new horoscopy based on genetic types – one that may at some future point regain some of the intellectual credibility that astrology enjoyed in its heyday.

The missing ship

One remarkable astrological success story comes from the annals of European overseas exploration. In 1519 the Portuguese navigator Ferdinand Magellan set off with five vessels under Spanish colours on an epic voyage that became the first circumnavigation of the world. Reaching the straits at the tip of South America that now bear his name, he stopped to wait for one of the vessels, the *San Antonio*, which had become separated from the rest of the fleet. After six days there was still no sign of the missing ship, so Magellan consulted the fleet's astrologer, Andreas de San Martin, to find out what had happened to it. San Martin consulted his charts and reported that the crew had mutinied, imprisoned their captain and turned back to Europe. Magellan proceeded with his journey westward, and although he was killed en route, one of his ships finally reached Spain after spending three years at sea. On their return the crew found that San Martin had been right – the *San Antonio* had indeed returned to Europe, and in just the way he had indicated.

the book of changes

The *Yi Jing* (Book of Changes) is one of the world's oldest divinatory texts, so ancient that its origins are thickly encrusted in legend. Its trigrams – sequences of three predictive lines, chosen by lot – are said to have been discovered by the legendary emperor Fu Xi, written on the back of a tortoise. In fact Fu Xi was a creature of myth, a culture hero with a serpent's body who reputedly taught the Chinese people the arts of cooking and fishing, so the name simply means "of immemorial antiquity".

Another heroic figure, this time from the shadowy border zone between legend and history, also supposedly played a part in shaping the work. This was Wen Wang, a leading figure in the reign of Zhou Xin, who was the last ruler of the Shang dynasty (ca. 1500–1045BCE) and a tyrant still remembered in China as the paradigm of sadistic power. Wen was not merely imprisoned by Zhou for suspected treason; on the emperor's orders he was also served the remains of one of his sons as soup. According to the story, Wen put his time in prison to use by coupling up the eight *Yi Jing* trigrams to form the 64 "hexagrams" that are the basis of the oracle to this day. In time another of Wen's sons, Prince Wu, overthrew Zhou Xin to found a new dynasty, the Western Zhou (ca. 1045–771BCE). Wu subsequently added to his father's work 384 commentaries that have since become an integral part of the *Yi Jing*.

So much for legend. In fact archeology has provided insights into the real-life background to the *Yi Jing* in the form of more than 100,000 "oracle bones". These show that China had a long tradition of divination stretching back into the New Stone Age (7000–1500BCE). The preferred method of the early diviners was to heat animal bones – particularly shoulder blades – or tortoise shells over fire and to predict the future from the random pattern of cracks that appeared. The system, known as scapulomancy, may have derived from sacrificial rites in which priests pored over the bones of the offerings for signs that they had been acceptable to the gods. It became customary in time for diviners to annotate the readings. These annotations have provided posterity with a record of the chief concerns of the forecasters and their clients at an extremely early time, for most of the surviving bones date from 1400–1100BCE. This was the Bronze

The symbols the ancient diviners scrawled on oracle bones such as this Shang-dynasty (ca. 1500–1045BCE) example are thought to have played a significant part in the development of Chinese writing.

Age era when, far away to the west, the Mycenean kings of Greece were caught up in the power struggles that ultimately led to the siege of Troy.

The oracle bones show that many consultations were religious, concerned with finding suitable times for making sacrifice. Others dealt with the likelihood of rain or wind, and the prospects for the forthcoming harvest. Many more set out to answer questions affecting the king or other members of the ruling house. Some were general forecasts of future events. Others addressed specific queries about the likely outcome of hunting trips, military excursions or proposed new settlements.

Consulting the *Yi Jing*

Scapulomancy as practised in ancient China was obviously an expensive business, aimed at a largely royal or aristocratic clientele. It may be that the *Yi Jing*, which

A bronze tortoise statue from the palace complex in Beijing known as the Forbidden City. Fu Xi is said to have discovered the predictive trigrams of the Yi Jing written on the back of a tortoise – the connection indicates a genuine line of descent from early forms of tortoise-shell divination.

was evidently formulated in the first half of the first millennium BCE, initially won favour by broadening the market for divination beyond the ranks of those who could afford to pay for a sacrificial animal. To consult the *Yi Jing*, diviners needed no more than a knowledge of the hexagrams and a bunch of yarrow stalks, the traditional means of casting the lots on which the choice of hexagram, and hence the relevant reading, depended.

Consulting the *Yi Jing* seems to have changed little over the centuries. The yarrow-plant method, which

involves sorting a bundle of *Achillea millefolium* stalks
into two randomly divided piles, is still very much in
use. This method allows for some sleight of hand on the
diviner's part, which adds to the impressiveness of the
ritual. An easier system, which is just as consistent with
the philosophy underlying the oracle, uses three coins.
In either case, the aim is to end up with a set of numerical
values that can be represented in the hexagram as lines,
either solid or broken. In the coin oracle, for example,
heads count as two and tails as three, so each throw
produces a total between six and nine. Six throws of the
coins produce the six lines of the hexagram, which is
always constructed from the bottom up.

As a further sophistication, the straight and broken
lines forming the hexagram can be either strong or weak.
The strong lines – formed in the coin oracle by throwing
a six or nine, rather than the more common seven or
eight – are given special emphasis in interpreting the
results, and are considered to be "mature". In terms of
Chinese dualist philosophy, this implies that the lines

*A circle of interlocking yin-yang symbols ringed by the eight
trigrams of the Yi Jing looms over a guardian tiger. This red-lacquer
panel would have been hung on a door to keep evil spirits away.*

are in the process of transforming into their opposite. A second hexagram can thus be formed, in which "strong" solid lines are replaced by broken ones, and vice versa. This second hexagram is also taken into account in interpreting the reading.

Changing interpretations

The background to this procedure lies deep in traditional Chinese ways of thought. The notion underlying the oracle abandons Western concepts of causality in favour of a view that Carl Jung, who wrote a foreword for the English translation of the *Yi Jing* (see box, below), called "synchronicity" – the idea that every aspect of the universe at a particular moment in time is somehow interconnected. This viewpoint (though with a causal element implied) has achieved some popularity in the West in recent years through the chaos theory outlined by Edward Lorenz, a mathematician and meteorologist at the Massachussets Institute of Technology, in 1961. Famously, Lorenz coined the "butterfly-effect" metaphor, suggesting that a butterfly flapping its wings in the Brazilian rain forest could trigger a chain of events that might eventually lead to a tornado striking Texas.

Over the centuries, the *Yi Jing*'s trigrams were codified and reinterpreted in China according to the changing philosophical preoccupations of the day. Confucianism and Daoism, the two great philosophical systems of the first millennium BCE, both left their mark on the commentaries and interpretations that now form part of the oracle. The book's status was such that it ranks as one of the Five Classics that make up the canon of Confucian learning, and as such it has been pored over more intensely by students and scholars than any other divinatory work.

The Confucian influence can be seen in the way that the oracular responses are worded. They are presented not so much as forecasts of what will happen as in terms of advice to "the superior man", recommending how he should adjust his behaviour to affect a desirable outcome. The phraseology reflects Confucius's own concern with counselling a ruling class on whose wisdom and sound judgment, he believed, the good ordering of

society depended. Thanks to the Confucian input, the *Yi Jing* has a moral dimension lacking in other divinatory systems – it seeks to impart guidance alongside prognostications of future developments. In China itself some of the *Yi Jing*'s interpretations have in fact achieved the status of a wisdom literature.

The Daoist influence is even more marked. Whereas Confucian thought always stressed reason, order and morality, Daoism – as outlined by Laozi in the *Dao De Jing* – took a more mystical approach that emphasized being in tune with the universe and "going with the flow". The notions of *yin* and *yang* – the opposite but complementary forces of male and female, light and dark, action and passivity permeating the workings of the universe – were fundamental to Daoism, and they have also indelibly marked the *Yi Jing*. The eternal movement of *yin* into *yang* and back again explains not just the duality of solid and broken lines in the trigrams but also the transition of strong lines into their opposites. The world of the *Yi Jing* is one of constant flux; in a universe in which transformation is the eternal norm, a wise person must learn to adapt to change like a skilled surfer constantly balanced on the edge of a rolling wave.

carl jung and the *yi jing*

The great Swiss psychiatrist Carl Jung encouraged the publication of the *Yi Jing* in the West and wrote a foreword for the English translation in 1949. In doing so, he revealed that he had consulted the oracle himself as to the wisdom of the move. It responded with the hexagram denoting the Cauldron, an image of a ritual vessel containing cooked food. Jung took the vessel to symbolize the *Yi Jing* itself, and the food the spiritual nourishment that it contained. In one respect the oracle was indisputably appropriate: the judgment associated with the hexagram is "Supreme good fortune. Success". The publication not only became a longterm best-seller but also helped to establish the *Yi Jing*'s popularity in the USA and Europe.

The Druids

Early antiquaries believed that southern England's Stonehenge (left) was a druid temple, and it is still celebrated as such by some to this day. However, most modern scholars note that the druids seem to have performed many of their rites in forest groves.

In pre-Christian times the druids were the priestly class of the Celtic peoples of western Europe. Relatively little is known about them, because they did not put their beliefs in writing. Although some inferences can be made from surviving Celtic myth and poetry, most of the information that survives comes from foreign, often distinctly hostile observers. The major sources are the Roman historians, particularly Julius Caesar, who took a personal interest in the druids in the first century BCE. He reported that they were held in high esteem in the Celtic lands, ranking alongside the military chiefs in public regard. Besides performing sacrifices and other religious duties, they served as teachers and as magistrates. They carried in their memories a vast store of oral knowledge that could take 20 years or more to learn. They

were absolved from all military duties and they paid no taxes.

One other firmly-established fact is that the druids practised divination and prophecy. The Roman statesman and essayist Cicero, a contemporary of Caesar, reported a conversation with a druid who claimed he could foretell the

future "sometimes through augury and sometimes by conjecture". There are accounts, too, of Roman leaders consulting female druids. Diocletian was told, "When you have killed the boar, you will be emperor" – a prediction that was fulfilled after the death of his enemy, the prefect Aper, whose name meant "the Boar".

How the druids practised divination is rather less clear. One strand evidently came from the close observation of nature. Trained druids were said to be able to foretell the future from the shapes of clouds

The Salmon of Knowledge

An Irish myth that may have some bearing on druidical notions of divination describes how the hero, Finn mac Cumhaill, was apprenticed as a child to a bard to learn the art of poetry. Finn's mentor spent his days on the banks of the River Boyne, seeking to catch a magical salmon that was said to have fed in its youth on nuts from the Tree of Knowledge. It was foretold that whoever should eat the fish would receive the gift of foreknowledge. Eventually the older man succeeded in landing the salmon, and passed it to his apprentice for cooking. As Finn was grilling the fish, a blister appeared on its skin, and the boy used his thumb to burst it, burning himself as he did so. To ease the pain he sucked his thumb – and so became the first person to taste the salmon's flesh, and thus the beneficiary of its wisdom.

or the flight of birds. There is a reference to captive hares being released so that druids could study the course they took to determine the outcome of a battle. A form of scapulomancy also seems to have been practised on the bones of the sacrificial animals, and there are reports of seers cracking open the bones of dogs, cats and pigs to taste the marrow.

Ritually killed beasts also feature in a form of dream oracle that was practised in the Celtic lands. According to the first-century BCE Greek historian Diodorus Siculus, a druid would chew a small piece of the flesh of a pig or horse and place it on a flagstone by the door of the house where he was resting, apparently as an offering to the gods. He would then sink into a deep sleep, in the course of which a totemic animal would appear to him to answer questions about the future. There are similar reports of a ceremony known as "bull sleep", in which the diviner slumbered on a tanned bull's hide in quest of prophetic dreams. Other sources talk of individuals being taken into dark places and kept in a state of sensory deprivation for hours or even days; when they were led into the light, they were expected to make inspired utterances.

One odd form of divination was the so-called "meditation on the finger-ends", which involved drumming and chanting to empower the fingertips to sense knowledge of the past or future in a person or object they subsequently touched.

The Bard, *painted by John Martin ca. 1817, shows a Welsh druid standing on a clifftop. He is calling down curses on the army of the 13th-century king Edward I, who annexed Wales to the English crown, passing below.*

ROMAN AUGURY

A wallpainting of a seer paying homage at the door of the Underworld from the 6th-century BCE Etruscan Tomb of the Auguries in Tarquinia. The Romans enthusiastically embraced Etruscan augury. As early as 304 BCE, there is a record of Roman aristocrats sending their sons to study divination in Etruria, in the hope that the knowledge they gained would help them in their careers.

The Roman state had the distinction of setting up what amounted to a bureaucracy of divination. Behind Roman augury lay the idea that the familiar pantheon of gods – Jupiter, Mars, Apollo and so on – controlled the physical aspects of the natural world, and could, if they wished, use it to communicate by means of omens. The signs could be either natural, such as eclipses or lightning flashes, or artificially induced, as when augurs seeking to know the divine will released sacred chickens and watched their feeding patterns. In either case it behoved prudent

individuals, as well as the rulers of a well-run state, to keep a close watch over such portents to check whether their actions were in accord with the will of the gods. Roman augury, in its organization and its intentions, was the most practical kind of divination, designed not so much to penetrate the veils of the future – for that the Romans relied, like the Greeks (see pages 22–7) on dreams, oracles or the utterances of inspired seers – as to learn whether a specific course of action could expect to win the favour of the relevant god.

The Etruscan legacy

The methods used by the Romans to determine the divine will were, for the most part, borrowed from their northern neighbours, the Etruscans. Rome conquered Etruria in the course of the fifth century BCE, and subsequently accepted its people as fellow-citizens. The Etruscans were famed for their skill in divination, and despite some misgivings – Cicero would one day write that "the entire Etruscan nation has gone stark mad on the subject of entrails" – the Romans proved happy to take advantage of their expertise.

Etruscan divination was a matter for experts. There was a myth to explain how they originally came by their knowledge. It described how a marvellous child, Tages, had sprung fully formed and with the face of a wizened old man from a furrow in a field near the town of Tarquinia. The startled ploughman quickly spread the word, and a large crowd gathered to see the marvel. Tages proceeded to expound many mysteries to his audience including the secrets of divination, and these were carefully copied down by Etruscan scribes. Then, with his mission accomplished, he vanished quite as suddenly as he had first appeared.

The Romans not only took over the knowledge passed down from Tages, but also formalized it and put it to the service of the state as part of their remorseless drive for efficiency and power. They made a distinction between auspices (*auspicia*), which were messages in the natural world to be deciphered, and portents (*prodigia*), unusual phenomena indicating that one of the gods was angry and therefore needed to be appeased.

Auspices came in various forms, but the principal ones were sky signs, such as lightning flashes and the behaviour of birds. These were the special domain of the augurs, officials who were appointed for life. From three or four in early republican times, their numbers rose to 16 by Julius Caesar's day in the first century BCE. Their staff of office was the bent stave known as the *lituus*, and they were conspicuous in togas striped in scarlet and edged with purple. The augurs were high officers of state whose advice had to be sought before any major public decision could be taken. They had real power, too, for they had only to declare that the omens were unfavourable to indefinitely suspend such major matters as elections, consecrations or even declarations of war.

The Roman Liver of Piacenza is a bronze model of a sheep's liver marked up for the haruspex's reading (see page 86). Livers were examined in search of a sign from the deity to whom the sacrifice had been made. This form of divination is known as extispicy.

The augurs exercised their duties from consecrated ground, the so-called *templum* or sanctuary, which they could create by simply outlining a space around themselves with their wands. From within this area they studied the skies, for flights of birds by day and at night for lightning and other signs. Their method of operation involved mentally dividing the sky, first into quarters along the major compass lines and then into sixteenths. The Etruscans, from whom the practice derived, had associated each section with an individual god. The significance of a given flock of birds or flash of lightning would differ markedly depending on its position in the sky. In general terms, signs in the east were taken as favourable and those in the west as inauspicious, while those in the north were held to have a particularly portentous significance.

The art of the haruspex

Portents could come in many forms, from earthquakes and volcanic eruptions to the appearance of freaks: monstrously deformed children, calves with two heads and the like. Such apparitions were considered deeply ominous, indicating that peaceful relations with the gods were under strain, and in serious cases the Senate would be consulted to determine the correct response. Usually

the matter would be delegated to the haruspices, often referred to generically as "Etruscans", as so many of them came from that region. When these expert diviners had reported back, expiatory rituals to appease the god – usually special prayers or sacrifices – would be announced.

The haruspices were not, at least until imperial times, state officials in the way that the augurs were. However, they were held in high esteem, and were consulted by private individuals as well as by officials. Their speciality was examining the entrails of sacrificial animals, most often sheep or oxen, for signs that might show the will of the god to whom the sacrifice had been addressed. In particular, they studied the liver. The shape, colour and markings of this organ were all important, and particular attention was paid to the lobe, a pyramid-shaped projection known to the Romans as the *processus pyramidalis*. If this was large and well-formed, the signs were propitious, but a cleft or deformed example was distinctly ominous (see illustration, page 85).

The best-known example of Roman divination featured a haruspex. This was the warning given by Vestricius Spurrina to Julius Caesar before his assassination in the year 44 BCE. Caesar, who had recently routed the forces of his rival Pompey in a three-year civil war, was ruling Rome as a dictator, a position that had roused the bitter hostility of his political opponents. Before an important meeting of the Senate on the Ides of March (15 March) that Caesar was due to attend, various portents were noted: wild birds had roosted in the Forum, fiery apparitions had been seen fighting in the sky. Investigating these prodigies, Spurrina examined the liver of a sacrificial bull and found it severely deformed – reportedly, it had no lobe at all. Alarmed, he warned Caesar to beware the fateful gathering. Caesar, however, chose to ignore the advice and was assassinated as he entered the Senate for the meeting.

An imprudent commander

Roman military forces on campaign favoured augury based on the feeding patterns of chickens. The answers to the diviner's questions depended on the order in which the chickens chose to feed on an area divided into segments. In 249 BCE, before the sea battle of Drepanum fought against the Carthaginian fleet, the admiral Claudius Pulcher became so infuriated by the refusal of the sacred chickens to eat the grain provided for them that he seized the birds and hurled them into the sea, saying "If they won't eat, let them drink!" Pulcher's forces were roundly defeated in the ensuing engagement, and he was charged with treason.

Despite their occasional successes, not all Romans were impressed by the haruspices' skills; in the second century BCE, the orator Cato the Elder remarked that it was beyond him how one haruspex could meet another and keep a straight face. There were stories, too, of occasional fraud: a practitioner named Soudinos was accused of inscribing "Victory to the king" in reverse writing on his palm, so that after he had handled the liver the words appeared, as if miraculously, imprinted on its surface.

The soothsayers' concern with the bloodier portions of sacrificial beasts may now seem distasteful, but it had a long pedigree, stretching back beyond Etruscan times to the earliest days of divination in Babylon. A modern researcher, Robert Temple, who obtained lambs' livers from an abattoir in the manner of the Roman diviners, has reported that they are perfectly shiny for the first 15 or 20 minutes following their removal from the body, after which they cloud over. Temple suggests that this striking initial clarity may have led ancient diviners to regard livers in the most literal sense as divine mirrors reflecting the will of the god.

A world full of omens

Roman soothsaying was by no means limited to the official or semi-official pronouncements of the augurs and haruspices. Private citizens also took advantage of various alternative sources of advice, ranging from oracles and prophetic dreams to dice-throwing and other forms of casting lots. The Romans saw omens in everyday mishaps such as stumbling, sneezing or the accidental spilling of salt. Yet Rome's most distinctive contribution to the history of divination undoubtedly lay in the practicality of its approach and its subjection of divination to the greater good of the state. In this field, as in so many others, the Roman talent for efficient organization is what shines through.

the tarot

Tarot cards are probably the most common divinatory accessories in the West today, rivalled in popularity only by the *Yi Jing* (see pages 78–81). The basic tarot deck consists of 78 cards. Fifty-six of these – the so-called Minor Arcana – are arranged in four suits: Cups, Coins, Swords and Batons. Each suit contains 14 cards (one more than in the standard Western 52-card deck). The extra one is an additional court card, the Knight, which fits between Queen and Jack. The remaining 22 cards form the Major Arcana. These are a series of picture cards, each bearing the image of a symbolic figure: the Sun, Justice, Death and others. Twenty-one of these cards are numbered, from 1 (the Magician) to 21 (the World). The 22nd is the Fool, who performs a function similar of that of the Joker in the modern Western pack.

To tell fortunes with the tarot, the reader may lay out the cards in any one of innumerable patterns, in each of which the position of a card affects its meaning. One of the most popular spreads is the Celtic cross, which employs 10 cards chosen at random after the person consulting the tarot (the querent) has shuffled the deck. The reader then lays the first card face down in the centre of the table, placing a second card horizontally across it –

The Hanged Man, from a tarot deck thought to have been painted by a Ferrarese artist in about 1480. In Renaissance times, the figure of a man hanged upside down by one foot represented the Traitor. Today the card is usually linked with sacrifice and waiting.

> "when a man is fully initiated he has a knowledge of all those processes [transmutation], and he knows that he holds those secrets under the penalty of death."

(ELIPHAS LEVI ON THE HANGED MAN, SAID TO REPRESENT THE NEED FOR SILENCE BY TRUE ADEPTS OF THE TAROT)

these two represent respectively the central issue raised by the consultation and any crossing influences that may affect it. Four cards are then laid around these two, starting from the bottom and working clockwise – these in turn reflect the situation's longterm background, the recent past, the possible outcome and the near future. Finally, the remaining four cards are laid out to the side of the cross, starting close to the reader and working in line upward. In sequence, they describe the influence on the situation of the querent, of other people, the querent's hopes and fears, and finally the likely outcome. A tarot consultation thus involves an in-depth analysis of a given situation. The individual is forced to consider his or her position from many points of view, almost regardless of the cards that are turned up.

The new game

As for the cards themselves, much nonsense has been written about their supposed antiquity, which the British scholar Michael Dummett has sought to demystify. In his 1980 work *The Game of Tarot*, he showed that the deck originated as just that – a card game, based on taking tricks. The tarot was in fact invented in fifteenth-century Italy, and for more than 300 years after the game's first appearance there is no known reference to it – or, indeed, to any pack of cards – being used for the purposes of divination. Cartomancy (fortune-telling by cards) seems, in the West at least, to have been an eighteenth-century innovation (although there may have been an earlier tradition of cartomancy that went unnoticed in the literature). Very soon after cartomancy was introduced the first esoteric claims were made for the tarot pack, deriving its symbolism supposedly from ancient Egypt.

There is, in fact, no evidence of any link with remote antiquity. The earliest surviving cards come from a set hand-painted for a Duke of Milan in the 1440s. The first playing cards had reached Europe from the Islamic east some 60 years previously. The earliest reference to them

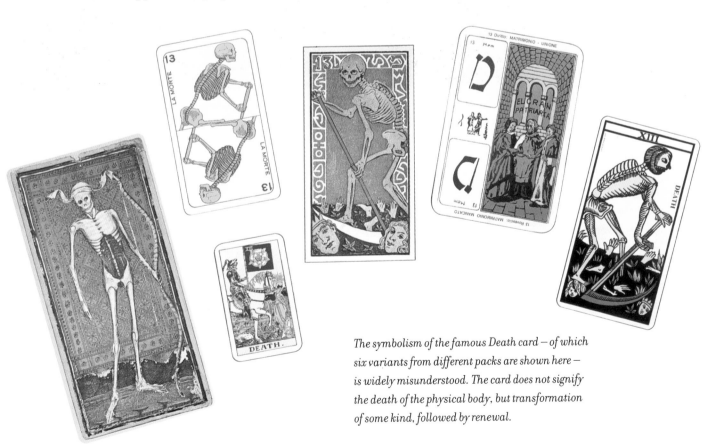

The symbolism of the famous Death card – of which six variants from different packs are shown here – is widely misunderstood. The card does not signify the death of the physical body, but transformation of some kind, followed by renewal.

Flemish artist Lucas van Leyden's The Card Reader, *painted in about 1508, shows a woman using cards either to tell fortunes or else to perform card tricks. At the same time, she is handing a flower to the nobleman on her left, while a second woman, standing to the right behind her, gives a fool a glass of wine. The painting has a moral — no-one is safe from foolishness and flattery.*

comes in a letter written in 1377 from a Swiss monastery by a German monk, who speaks of a new game that "reached us this year". The earliest known packs are in fact identical to the Minor Arcana of the tarot deck, having four suits with 14 cards in each one.

The suit names derived directly from the ones in use in Islamic countries at the time — coins, cups, swords and polo sticks (the polo sticks were changed to batons, as the game of polo was then unknown in the West). Hearts, diamonds, clubs and spades — the suits of the familiar 52-card deck — were a later invention, only introduced in about 1480. These new suits, which were devised mainly to make printing easier, only caught on in western Europe. Cups, coins, swords and batons are still the suits familiar to most card-players in southern Europe to this day.

What was new in the tarot pack, then, was the addition of the 22 cards of the Major Arcana to the existing deck commonly used at the time. Their function is suggested by their original name: *triunfi* or "triumphs", anglicized as "trumps". They were numbered from 1 to 21 not in pursuit of some deep, symbolic meaning, but simply to indicate which of the cards would outbid another.

The game proved instantly popular and remained so; it is played in Austria and central Europe to this day. Oddly, one of the few places where the game never caught on was Britain. In time, the tarot went out of fashion in Paris, so that when it was reintroduced to the French capital in the late eighteenth century it had an exotic allure that lent itself to arcane interpretations.

Cartomancy becomes fashionable

The divinatory tarot was very much the creation of the pre-revolutionary Paris of the late eighteenth century, where bored aristocrats were constantly on the look-out for new amusements. A taste for the exotic was in the air, fed by a fascination with the occult and also by a vogue for ancient Egypt, whose wonders were at the time gradually being revealed. As it happened, the tarot's new, esoteric reputation would manage to satisfy both appetites at once.

Three men played crucial roles in giving the cards their fresh significance. One was a print-seller named Alliette, who wrote books under the pseudonym of Etteilla — his own name spelled backward. One such, published in 1770, was itself entitled *Etteilla, or A Way to Amuse Oneself with Cards*, and it proposed a way of laying out cards to tell fortunes — a new form of recreation.

Etteilla's original system had no connection with the tarot, which was only reintroduced to Paris some years later. When the game reappeared, however, it rapidly caught the attention of an author named Antoine Court de Gebelin, who had long been a proponent of mystical theories about ancient Egypt. According to his own account, he happened one day upon some ladies playing the game at a salon, and on inspecting the cards instantly realized that they represented a forgotten lexicon of ancient Egyptian symbolism — one that had somehow survived through the millennia in the innocuous disguise of a parlour game. In fact it now seems likely that the idea was not Court de Gebelin's own. He had got it from a correspondent, who signed himself only as the Comte

de M, who sometime previously had sent him an essay describing the tarot as the lost *Book of Thoth*, the Egyptian god associated with magic. After Court de Gebelin published his discovery, Etteilla reappeared on the scene, adapting his earlier book to accommodate the new fashion. By the time Etteilla died in 1791, the myth of the tarot's ancient roots was already firmly implanted.

In the ensuing decades the theory of the tarot's Egyptian origins gradually fell out of favour, but other, equally exotic interpretations took its place. The French occultist Eliphas Levi linked the pack with the ancient Jewish mystical system known as the Cabala, ingeniously identifying the 22 cards of the Major Arcana with the 22 letters of the Hebrew alphabet. From France the occult tarot's popularity spread in time to England, where members of the mystical sect known as the Order of the Golden Dawn read into it a Christian symbolism based on Arthurian legend and the quest for the Holy Grail. Since then fresh theories and reinterpretations have proliferated: today there are Aztec, Norse and Native American tarot decks on the market.

Amid all the historical detective work and the deflating of untenable theories, it is quite easy to forget just how mysterious and evocative the Major Arcana cards actually are. Some of their strangeness can be put down to the passage of time. We still recognize instantly the figure of Justice in a woman with a sword and a pair of scales. Other images, such as the Papess or the Tower struck by lightning, remain unexplained. The tarot still has mysteries to reveal.

The Tarot of the Gypsies

The idea that gypsies have for many centuries used the tarot for purposes of divination is a myth of fairly recent origin. There is indeed an ancient gypsy tradition of fortune-telling, but one based on palmistry, not on playing cards. The earliest references to gypsies using the tarot in fact long postdate printed claims that they did so, made by occultist authors eager to establish the pack's oriental connections. Although there are now gypsy card-readers, it seems that they may have initially picked up the habit to meet the expectations of non-gypsies.

african divination

Across Africa's vast expanses practically every form of divination known to humankind is or has been practised. One source lists more than 60 different methods, and it is almost certainly not comprehensive. The old shamanism tradition (see pages 10–11) of individuals entering trances to consult the spirit world is alive and well, and is used particularly to trace the causes of illness and to detect hostile witchcraft. There are augurs who, like the ancient Romans (see pages 84–7), seek omens by studying the stars or watching the flight of birds. Various forms of scrying involving water-filled bowls are used, and there are elaborate systems for casting lots that rival the *Yi Jing* (see pages 78–81) in their complexity. In the past there were even formal oracles like the one at Delphi (see pages 24–7). A famous oracle at Aro Chuku in Nigeria was closed down by the British colonial authorities in 1900 when it was proved that unsuccessful applicants were being "disappeared" by the priests in charge. The victims, supposedly consumed by an angry god, were actually sold into slavery at the port of Bonny, 80 miles (130 km) to the south.

The clientele which consults the diviners is also varied, ranging from tribal chiefs eager to know the best time to perform a ritual observance or begin the harvest to individuals who have suffered misfortune or illness or are simply worried about their future prospects. Problems such as infertility, sick cattle and possession by hostile spirits might all be referred to a diviner, whose role in African traditional societies often parallels that of doctors and psychiatrists in the West.

Oracular animals

One technique that enjoys an unusual degree of popularity is animal divination. The Azande people, who straddle the border of Sudan and the Central African Republic, use termites' nests as a simple form of oracle. To settle a question with two possible outcomes, Azande diviners stick two branches into the nest, one on each side, and leave them overnight. The outcome depends on which of the two branches the termites choose to eat. If neither branch is touched, the question is thought to have been refused by the spirits.

A more complex tradition is passed on by the Dogon people, who live south of the River Niger in Mali. In their case the oracular animal is the sand fox, a shy nocturnal

A Dogon diviner from Mali. Having raked out a grid in the earth, the diviner is marking the grid's patches with a complex set of signs — twigs may be used to represent men and grass stalks women, charcoal for magic spells and small mounds of earth for the presence of evil.

predator that haunts the outskirts of their villages. Diviners have regular plots that they rake into grids. These are in turn subdivided into small patches, each of which serves to answer an individual question. Having prepared the grid, the diviner chants an invocation to the fox and the spirit it represents – for the animal is said to "talk to the spirit" – and then strews peanuts as bait on the borders between patches.

The next morning he (most of the diviners are men) will return to survey the outcome. If no fox has come or bad weather has obliterated the markings, then the reading is null and void. However, the diviner is usually able to trace the fox's pawprints across the various patches and, in the manner of a Roman augur inspecting the tracks of feeding chickens, will provide answers for his client's questions from the marks that the animal has made.

Throwing for the spirits

In southern Africa there is a long-established tradition of casting bones that stretches back to the culture that created Great Zimbabwe and probably much further. One popular system employs four bones – actually, the lots may equally well be made of ivory, horn or wood – which, when thrown, can give a total of 16 possible responses to queries. Each of the bones has a separate identity: male or female, senior or junior. Other diviners use a much greater number of knucklebones (up

An ivory tapper, or divination wand, from the Yoruba ifa *divination cult. The* ifa *priest (babalawo) uses the tapper to summon and greet the gods.*

to 60 in some cases), although again each one has an individual significance. Readings take account of the way the lots fall and their relationship to one another. The cowrie-shell diviners who tell fortunes in West African marketplaces use a similar system.

Probably the best-known of all the African oracular traditions is the *ifa* system practised by the Yoruba people of western Nigeria, Benin and Togo. *Ifa* priests use palm nuts, which they cast from hand to hand over a sawdust-covered divining board, making annotations in the dust depending on how many of the nuts remain left in the original hand after each transmission. In all, eight markings are required, set out from right to left and downward in paired columns. The marks consist of either a single or double line, permitting 16 possible combinations. Each combination corresponds to one of the major *odu*, or divinatory spirits, sent down by the god Orunmila in ancient times to provide enlightenment for humankind. Once the relevant *odu* has been identified, the diviner and his client discuss the subject of the consultation in the light of the spirit's known divinatory attributes. The client thereby gets the benefit of the priest's long experience of similar problems, and the consoling knowledge that the spirit world too is concerned with its solution.

> "Heaven, come down to us. Make this house your home. Descend with complete power. Come, freshness, come!"
>
> (Invocation used by *ifa* priests in Nigeria to summon oracular spirits)

calendrical systems of mesoamerica

Over the centuries, peoples of many cultures have had systems for working out auspicious and inauspicious days. However, nowhere in the world have such schemes been taken to the extremes of complexity and sophistication that they attained in Mexico and Central America in the years before the Spanish conquest (see pages 56–7).

The peoples of the region, of whom the best known are the Aztecs and the Maya, shared many preconceptions about the passage of time. For all of them, calendars were an essential means of conceiving and organizing their world and of predicting its likely future course. To Mesoamerican eyes, calendars did far more than simply register the date. Each day was placed under a range of divine and astrological influences. Between them, these influences determined whether or not the day would be propitious, which helped dictate the activities that could be undertaken on it.

The Mesoamerican years

All the Mesoamerican nations recognized a 365-day annual cycle that corresponded approximately to our solar year. The year was divided into 18 months of 20 days, leaving a residue of five days at the end of each year. These so-called Nameless Days were regarded as unlucky because they were not under the protection of any god. However, the Mesoamerican peoples had no equivalent to our leap year, with the result that their 365-day reckoning gradually fell out of synchronization with the cycle of the seasons. This calendar was used for fixing public events, but its imprecision meant that sowing and harvest festivals,

The early 16th-century Aztec Calendar Wheel, or Sun Stone, is actually a stone representation of the Aztec cosmogony, incorporating 20 day signs and four panels for the previous world eras (see page 96).

for example, had periodically to be shifted to keep in calibration with the agricultural year.

The calendrical system that was of most account for purposes of divination was an entirely separate, 260-day year that ran in tandem with the 365-day reckoning. There is no obvious seasonal basis for this second cycle. The most likely link seems to be with the human gestation period, measured from the first missed menstrual cycle to birth – midwives may have used a 260-day count to calculate the expected date of delivery. Evidence supporting this view comes from the fact that Aztec children generally took their names from their birth date as measured by this count, and were thought to have already completed one cycle by the time they were born.

The names children were given combined one of 20 day-names, such as Wind, Deer, Flint or Flower, with a repeating cycle of 13 numbers. For example, a person might be called Two Deer or Twelve Flint. For the Aztecs, each of the 20 names was associated with a specific god, as were the 13 numbers, their patrons being the 13 Lords of the Day. There were also other influences at work, for example 13 flying creatures, ranging from hummingbirds to owls, which in turn were each related to one of the 13 levels of the Aztec Heaven. As a result, the 260-day calendar was the ultimate diviner's almanac, providing a complex tangle of different influences for every day that only a specialist could unravel. In fact, all Aztec priests received instruction in divination.

The Caracol in the ruined Maya city of Chichén Itzá in northern Yucatán, Mexico. The building is thought to have served as an observatory to chart the movements of Venus.

"[The 260-day calendar] taught the indian nations the days on which they were to sow, reap, till the land, cultivate corn, weed, harvest, store, shell the ears of corn, sow beans and flax seed."

(THE SPANISH CHRONICLER FRA DIEGO DURAN ON THE MESOAMERICAN CALENDAR'S ROLE IN FIXING PROPITIOUS TIMES FOR ALL ACTIVITIES)

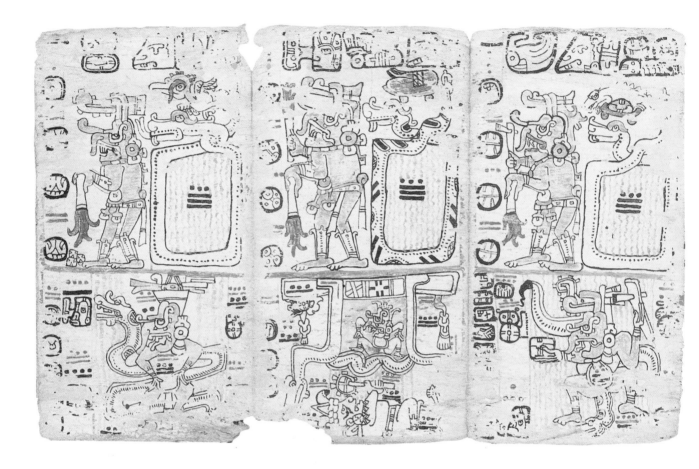

Certain days had a lingering influence that extended well beyond the 24-hour period they actually covered. A person's birthname could affect his or her fortune for life, so children born on unpropitious days were often renamed later on a more auspicious one.

The sacred cycle

Both the Aztecs and the Maya had a sophisticated knowledge of mathematics, and were profoundly aware of the numerical patterns underlying the meshing of the two calendars. They had worked out that it took 18,980 days — 73 years by the 260-day count, and 52 years by the 365-day one — for the two calendars to coincide. In Mesoamerican culture, this 52-year period assumed great importance. It was known as the "bundle of years", so called from the priests' habit of setting aside a peeled wooden wand to mark each new year. When 52 wands had been assembled, the period known to modern historians as the "calendar round" had come full circle.

For the Aztecs, the end of any cycle was a dangerous period when, briefly, the world ceased to be under the protective influence of the usual gods. As a result, the conclusion of

The "Madrid" Maya codex was compiled in the 15th century, probably in Yucatán. It contains descriptions of the divinities linked with each day of the sacred calendar.

the calendar round was a time of particular terror. According to the Aztecs' cosmogony, the world had been created and destroyed four times before the fifth sun had risen on the present age, and they expected this epoch too to pass away, after which no further suns would rise. Their only certainty about the timing of the end of the world was that it would happen at the end of a calendar round, although no-one knew which one. Therefore, each time the fateful moment came around, there was real fear of cosmic disaster and a nagging worry that the gods might choose the occasion to finally sweep away all traces of their human creation.

To minimize the risks, an important ritual known as the New Fire Ceremony was performed. On the last day of the 52-year calendar round people smashed all their household crockery and extinguished all fires. Normal daily life came to a halt, and fasting, abstinence and silence were the order of the day. After night had fallen, a procession of priests and dignitaries made their way out of the Aztec capital of Tenochtitlán to the top of a nearby mountain, known as Citlaltepec or "Hill of the Star". There they waited tensely to see if the constellation we know as the Pleiades would stand revealed at midnight — a sight taken to confirm that the world would continue into a new cycle. When the stars had duly been sighted, the priests sacrificed a human victim — usually an enemy general taken as a prisoner of war — cutting his heart out with a flint knife. They then used fire sticks to rekindle within the dead man's exposed breast a spark, from which they lit brands that were waved to signal the good news of the world's deliverance to the anxious citizens watching far below. A wave of relief and rejoicing then spread through the capital and the entire Aztec world, for the demons of destruction had been kept at bay once more, and humankind was guaranteed survival for at least another 52 years.

Maya calendars

Caught up in this recurrent pattern of fear and salvation, the Aztecs had no measure for time that stretched beyond the 52-year limit. This was a defect that the Maya, who had flourished some centuries earlier in what are now southern Mexico and Guatemala, had remedied by the invention of the dizzyingly lengthy cycle known as the Long Count (see box, below). The Maya calendrical system was even more complex than the Aztec one, for in addition to the 260- and 365-day years, Maya priests also calculated a lunar calendar reckoned from the first appearance of each new moon. They kept sufficiently precise records to calculate that 149 moons equated to the passage of 4,400 days, giving an average length for each lunar cycle of 29.5302 days. The accepted figure for a lunar cycle today is 29.5306.

The Maya had their own almanac of influences for each day of the year, rather different in its details from that of the northern peoples. They also recognized other cycles as well, paying particular attention to the rising of Venus, which they identified with military activity — their glyph for "war" represented Venus over the symbol for the place attacked. The Maya often timed assaults to coincide with the planet's first rising as the Evening Star.

The End of the Maya Long Count

To calculate the passage of time over lengthy periods, the Maya devised the Long Count, which reckoned events from a fixed date in the distant past when, according to their reckoning, the present era of the world had begun. In Western terms, the count started on 11 August 3114BCE. There are no surviving records to explain why that date was chosen, but some artwork suggests that it might have marked the recreation of the world after its destruction by a great flood.

Long Count years were measured in *tuns* of 360 days. In line with Maya vigesimal mathematics — based on the number 20 rather than the decimal system's 10 — longer periods were measured in terms of the *katun* (20 *tuns*) and *baktun* (20 *katuns*, or 400 *tuns*). Even longer stretches of 20 and 400 *baktuns* were also taken into account, defining eras of respectively 8,000 and 160,000 *tuns*.

Like all other Mesoamerican calendars, the Long Count itself was a cycle and was scheduled to have an end, expected after 13 *baktuns* had expired. Allowing for Western calendrical adjustments and the discrepancy between the 360- and 365-day year, that date falls due on 21 December 2012 when, if the Maya got their calculations right, the present cycle of existence should come to an end.

The scryer's art

Scrying is one of the oldest and most far-flung divinatory methods. The word – which comes from the verb "to descry", meaning to observe – covers a gamut of ways of seeking knowledge by staring fixedly at smooth or reflective surfaces – typically glass balls, but also crystals and still water among other options. Scrying's history stretches back at least as far as classical Greece, where the travel writer Pausanias described several springs used for such purposes. One, at Taenarum near the Peloponnese's southernmost tip, supposedly revealed whatever was happening in the local harbour until a local woman polluted it by washing dirty clothes in its waters. In the Bible, the book of Genesis has a reference to Joseph's use of a divining cup, while Islamic tradition holds that the eighth-century Abbasid caliph al-Mansur had a mirror that miraculously revealed whether strangers were friends or enemies.

In Mesoamerica scrying seems to have played a particularly prominent role, represented by its association with Tezcatlipoca (see pages 56–7), a fearsome deity whose name meant "smoking mirror". Statues of the god show just such a mirror, made of the dark volcanic rock obsidian, decorating the back of his head, while a second often replaces one of his feet, lost while battling the earth monster in a creation struggle. The Aztecs are known to have used such mirrors for divination, along with bowls of water. Allied beliefs evidently percolated south through the Isthmus of Panama to Peru, to judge from a famous Inca legend describing how the conqueror Pachacuti found in a stream a piece of crystal in which the figure of the creator god Viracocha appeared, promising him empire.

As these early examples indicate, there are many different forms of scrying, some more widespread than others. Nowadays most people associate the technique with crystal balls, but that has not always been so. Mirrors have as good a pedigree – the "mirror, mirror, on the wall" in the Snow White fairy story is a familiar

A 17th-century portrait of the English occultist John Dee. Having long experimented with astrology and alchemy, Dee turned to scrying relatively late in life. He saw in it a way of attaining levels of knowledge not available from conventional sources.

example from folktale – while the ancient Greeks were far from the only people to use the water of rivers, lakes or streams to serve as their speculum (the scryer's name for the object observed).

Other substances besides glass and water can also be put to use. Practitioners of lithomancy use shiny stones. One of the strangest methods, onychomancy, now probably defunct, involved studying the fingernails of a young boy, covered with soot and turned to the sun. In

> ## "ı had sight offered me in chrystallo; and ı saw."
>

recent times, scryers have reportedly got results from a range of unexpected objects, including soap bubbles, the backs of watches and blank television screens.

Scrying has been put to many purposes over the ages, including prophecy for prophecy's sake. An example from Saint-Simon's *Memoirs* describes a little girl who, simply by gazing into a glass of water, was able to describe many historical incidents that subsequently took place. However, from the early days other people have approached the glass with definite ends in view. Sometimes single people scried to see their future partner. There was an old North American folk tradition that a girl who went down a flight of stairs backward on Halloween while looking into a mirror would glimpse the face of her husband-to-be.

One tradition with a particularly long pedigree is the use of scrying to detect lost or stolen objects. The earliest reference to the practice in England dates from 1467, when a Yorkshireman named William Byg confessed to earning his living by using a crystal ball to trace lost property. Charged with heresy by the ecclesiastical authorities, he was sentenced to walk to York Minster bearing placards declaring him a sorcerer.

The Elizabethan scryer

Scrying could also be put, successfully or not, to more ambitious ends, as exemplified by the experiments of the sixteenth-century English occultist and scholar, John Dee. A man of great learning, Dee was well known to Queen Elizabeth I; he had even drawn up her horoscope. Indeed, some authorities think that he was

the model for Prospero in Shakespeare's *The Tempest*.

Long study of Jewish mystical lore had convinced Dee that a layer of angelic beings existed between man and God. In the 1580s Dee convinced himself that these spirits could be contacted through a crystal divining glass. Over the next decade he kept a diary of his experiments, documenting along the way one of the world's most extraordinary psychic adventure stories.

Sadly, Dee himself turned out to have little aptitude for summoning up spirits; "You know I cannot see or scry," he wrote despondently. As a result, he was forced to rely on assistants. By far the most significant was a quick-witted rogue named Edward Kelley, an adventurer who had already had his ears cropped for counterfeiting money in the years before Dee met him.

Not only did Kelley produce spirits thick and fast, he also summoned up a new divining ball for Dee in a highly

The crystal ball — or "shew stone", as he called it — thought to have belonged to John Dee.

dramatic fashion. Toward sunset one afternoon in 1582, Dee saw in the western window of his laboratory a vision of a child-angel, bearing in its hands "a bright object, clear and glorious, of the bigness of an egg". The crystal turned out to be real enough, and Dee would later describe it as the gift of Uriel, the angel of light.

However, Kelley was more interested in putting Dee's alchemical knowledge to use to make gold than in angelic spirits. In pursuit of this goal he persuaded the 56-year-old scholar to leave his home in Mortlake, outside London, and travel in company with his wife and

servants to Poland, where a wealthy nobleman had promised to support his researches. A six-year wild goose chase ensued that saw Dee and Kelley seeking favour not just in Poland but also at the Prague court of the Holy Roman Emperor Rudolf II and at the castle of the Viceroy of Bohemia. In the course of their wanderings, Kelley not only continued to summon angels and pursue alchemical researches, he also persuaded the ageing Dee that, on the advice of the spirits, the two men should share everything in common, including their wives. Meanwhile, rumours of Dee's

A hand-coloured engraving shows John Dee (1527–1608) and his associate Edward Kelley (born in 1555) supposedly raising a ghost in a moonlit graveyard.

magical activities sparked outrage back home, where an angry mob ransacked his house, burning many of his books and utensils.

Eventually Dee had had enough. He finally returned to England in 1589, bankrupt and disheartened. Fortunately for him, his old patron Queen Elizabeth took pity on his plight and rewarded his long service to the crown with the rectorship of a college in the growing northern town of Manchester.

Kelley was not so lucky. He stayed on in eastern Europe, where his welcome grew increasingly thin. Charged with fraud and sorcery, he was eventually thrown into prison. An attempted escape went disastrously wrong when the ladder of knotted sheets he was climbing down snapped under his weight, and he died from his injuries the following day. With him went the knowledge of whether he truly had seen wonders in the crystal ball. All that is known for certain is that Dee's subsequent experiments with scrying were unfruitful, and the angelic voices were stilled.

Cloudy visions

Today crystal-ball gazing remains the most popular scrying technique, although the modus operandi varies considerably between individual scryers. Some insist on several days' preparation to cleanse the body and the mind before they will attempt a séance, while others need no such preliminaries. Most insist that the speculum itself should be spotless and unflawed, as any imperfection in the glass can be distracting. A favourite cleaning method involves boiling the ball in a one-to-five mixture of brandy and water for 15 minutes and then drying it with a piece of chamois leather. Some diviners like to scry either in complete darkness or else against a dark background, such as a piece of velvet or a half-opened drawer. Others can work in broad daylight, although a majority prefer a dim light, with the ball positioned at typical reading distance away. In the past many diviners employed young boys or girls, who were thought to have particularly clear psychic vision, to look into the glass, limiting their own role to interpreting the visions that the youngsters reported seeing. However,

An Affair Revealed

A curious case of divinatory scrying was recorded in 1915 by a certain Dr Edmund Waller, who was living at the time in Paris. A friend going on a long trip to Africa asked him, as an act of kindness, to check that all was well with his wife while he was away. Soon after the friend's departure, however, the wife left for America, and Waller thought little more about his charge. Then, one night when he could not sleep, he decided for amusement to look into a crystal ball that his father had recently acquired. He was astonished to be greeted with a vision of the wife, in company with a man whom he did not know, in a setting that he recognized as the paddock of the Longchamps racecourse outside Paris. Realizing there was a meeting at Longchamps the following Sunday, he gave up an important engagement to be there, and duly saw the couple just as in his vision; the wife had evidently returned to France without his knowledge.

Subsequently he had several more crystal-ball sightings of the pair, which he duly reported to the woman's husband on his return to France. At first the man refused to believe the story. However, when Waller saw a fresh vision, this time of the couple in a well-known Parisian restaurant, the husband agreed to accompany him to the spot. They found the adulterous couple having dinner, and a scene ensued that eventually led to a divorce.

nowadays most do their own scrying. Typically, the vision itself may take 5 to 15 minutes to take shape.

What the scryer actually sees also varies between individuals, but the classic accounts speak of a milky or opaque cloud gradually filling the ball. The visions themselves appear out of this mist, often bathed in a preternaturally bright light. They may be still or moving, either circumscribed by the ball or else seemingly life-sized. Sometimes no shapes appear, yet the scryer may still garner some information from the clouds themselves; if they are light-coloured they generally denote good fortune, while dark hues imply foreboding.

A plethora of methods

Over the centuries human ingenuity has come up with innumerable ways of foretelling the future, most of them based solely on the chance coincidence of unconnected events. Lists of such divinatory techniques run quickly into the dozens, and sometimes to a hundred or more.

Some of the methods used are familiar to this day. Forms of palmistry were known to the Chinese and Indians thousands of years ago and are still popular now, having experienced a revival 100 or more years ago. This was partly thanks to the activities of the society clairvoyant Cheiro (born William Warner in County Wicklow, Ireland). Oneiromancy, the art practised by Joseph in Old Testament days (see pages 54–5), is also still flourishing, to judge from the number of dream books on offer in modern book-shops. Most people also have a passing acquaintance with aleuromancy, the custom of baking prophetic messages into cakes, if only in the debased modern form of fortune cookies.

Other entries on the lists now seem simply bizarre. Who practised

Exploiting the 19th-century fashion for phrenology, an American family named Fowler built a thriving business on offering cranial examinations and selling busts and charts like this one showing the activities associated with different areas of the brain.

cephalomancy, the custom of boiling donkeys' heads in water and predicting fate from the emerging bubbles? Gelomancy and gyromancy, which found omens respectively in hysterical laughter and the dizzy gait of whirling dancers, are both long gone. Playwrights and scriptwriters still perform a modified form of

transataumancy – seeking significance in overheard snippets of other people's conversations – but they put their findings to literary rather than prophetic use. Phrenology, which sought to identify an individual's character and capacities by examining the contours of his or her skull, has also gone out of fashion.

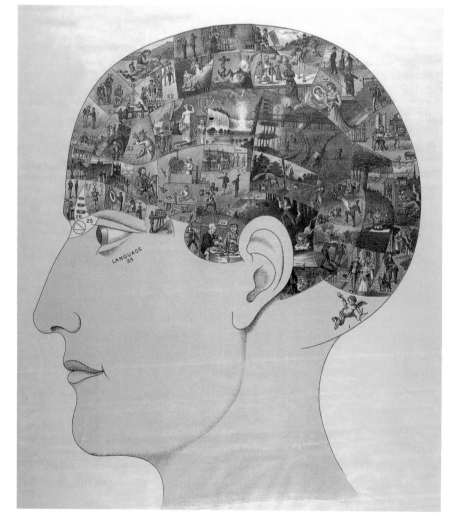

Pendulums and tea leaves

One old technique that has recently received a new lease of life is cleidomancy. As the name might suggest (*kleis* being Greek for "key"), this technique originally involved a key hanging on the end of a piece of string. Now, however, various kinds of bob replace the key, one popular choice being a quartz crystal at the end of a thread. Whatever the object, the aim is to make a pendulum that can be used for divination almost in the manner of a single-handed ouija board. Held motionless, the bob often appears to take on a life of its own, and the way in which it moves provides an answer to various types of query. It may serve in place of a dowsing wand to locate water or metal. Alternatively, the orientation of the swing can indicate the direction in which to look for lost objects. The pendulum can also be used to answer simple "Yes" or "No" to questions — if the bob rotates clockwise, the answer is taken to be "Yes", while counter-clockwise indicates "No". Needless to say, any slight tremor of the hand can set the pendulum moving, so the diviner needs to be firmly on guard against the danger of unconsciously determining the answer to his or her own query.

Of all the other traditional techniques, one that has the advantage of being immediately accessible as well as time-honoured is tasseomancy — the reading of the future from tea-leaves. Long a staple of gypsy fortune-telling,

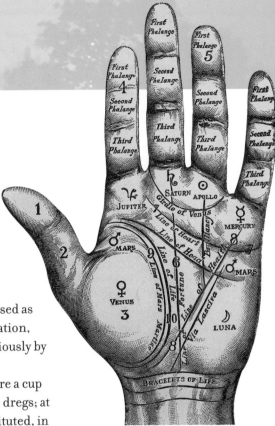

Palmistry is an ancient form of divination. Under the influence of the society clairvoyant Cheiro, it became highly popular in the 1890s, when this illustrated map of the hand was published.

tasseomancy is now widely used as a recreational form of divination, one that is not taken too seriously by most of its practitioners.

The only props needed are a cup of tea, drained almost to the dregs; at a pinch, coffee can be substituted, in which case one expert recommends that a mix of regular and fine grinds should be used for optimum pattern formation. The cup should be swirled vigorously to distribute the leaves, then turned upside down into the saucer to allow any remaining liquid to drain off. The process of divination involves examining the leaves left inside and using free association to identify shapes and patterns within them. There are few rules, except that proximity to the rim denotes closeness in time; a ship-shaped blob near the bottom of the cup would, for example, denote a sea journey in the distant future.

divination from books

One time-honoured form of divination by lottery is bibliomancy — telling the future by choosing passages at random from books. The Bible is a popular source, but historically it was eclipsed by the works of the Roman poet Virgil, whose esoteric reputation probably stemmed from the Underworld journey described in his masterpiece, *The Aeneid*. Virgil's poems were consulted for divinatory purposes even in classical times; reportedly the tough but effective emperor Septimus Severus fell on the line, "Never forget, O Roman, to rule the people with royal sway". There are also post-classical examples of appropriate choices. When King Charles I of England was persuaded to try this *sortes Virgilianae* (Virgilian lot-casting) sometime before the outbreak of the civil war that cost him his life in 1649, he came upon a passage from *The Aeneid*, Fourth Book, describing the coming of a war in which a king was killed.

seers and clairvoyants

Nostradamus is the arch-prophet, the secular seer all the world knows. Yet he also remains something of a mystery. Apart from some hints about the invocation of spirits, he kept his working methods to himself. There has never been a Nostradamian tradition of prophecy, because no-one knows for sure what exactly the great man did.

As such, Nostradamus makes a fitting patron for the clairvoyants assembled in this chapter, whose only common trait is their individuality. They range from the semi-mythical Merlin, whose legend draws on glimpsed memories of a real-life sixth-century seer, to Karl Ernst Krafft, whose strange story unfolded against the backdrop of the Nazi Third Reich. The cast of characters includes sophisticated thinkers such as the scholar-monk Roger Bacon, who foresaw elevators and aeroplanes 600 years before their time, but also such naturals as Robert Nixon, the Cheshire Idiot, whose clairvoyant powers were entirely spontaneous and uncontrolled, and Edgar Cayce, the American "sleeping prophet", who expected part of Atlantis to resurface in the 1960s. These are the great individualists of prophecy: each one was regarded as exceptional in his or her own time, and their memory has survived to the present day.

merlin the prophet

Merlin remains very much in the public eye today, thanks to Arthurian books and films. However, few people are aware of Merlin's origins as a prophet – and supposedly a historical one at that.

The celebrated wizard made his first appearance around the year 1135CE in Geoffrey of Monmouth's *Historia Regum Brittaniae* (History of the Kings of Britain), one of the most popular and influential books of the Middle Ages. Purporting to be a history of Britain from about 1170BCE until the eighth century CE, the contents of the book in fact came largely from Geoffrey's fertile imagination. Besides Merlin, the *Historia* also featured King Arthur, although in the book Merlin's only association with the monarch is to use his magic to help Arthur's father, Uther Pendragon, deceitfully to force his favours on Arthur's mother.

According to the *Historia*, Britain was originally peopled by followers of Brutus, the son of the Trojan hero Aeneas. Geoffrey then supplied an entire lineage of largely imaginary kings, including King Lear and Cymbeline, both familiar today from Shakespeare's plays. While acknowledging the Roman conquest, Geoffrey chose to portray the Romans as little more than shadowy overlords.

The most interesting and influential part of Geoffrey's work described events after the Romans'

Painted in 1874 by Sir Edward Burne-Jones, The Beguiling of Merlin *shows the wizard being seduced by the nymph Nimue.*

departure. According to Geoffrey, the throne of Britain was usurped by a treacherous interloper named Vortigern. Not only did he force the rightful heirs into exile, but he also invited heathen Saxons into the country as mercenaries to buttress his position.

According to the story, the Saxons liked what they saw of Britain, and in time turned their swords against Vortigern too. He retreated to the mountain fastness of Snowdonia, where he planned to build an impregnable stronghold. However, every attempt to construct it failed, for the walls kept falling down. Convinced that magic was at work, Vortigern summoned his soothsayers, who told him that the only way to counter the spell was to offer up for sacrifice a child who had been born without a father. Vortigern searched far and wide for such a prodigy. He finally found the young Merlin, whose mother had been made pregnant by an incubus, or spirit lover, rendering the boy fatherless in human terms.

However, Merlin also had prophetic powers, and before he could be sacrificed he insisted on challenging Vortigern's soothsayers to a contest of skill. After they had tried and failed to reveal the reason why the castle kept collapsing, Merlin successfully explained the mystery – they were building over an underground pool in which lived two warring dragons. Vortigern investigated, and duly found the dragons. One was red, one white, and they at once started to fight each other.

A prophetic history

Pressed for an explanation, Merlin responded with a long, prophetic speech that was celebrated throughout the Middle Ages as the "Prophecies of Merlin". It spelled out nothing less than a prophetic history of Britain, presented in allegorical terms and stretching over a period of a thousand years or more. The early part is obscure but occasionally strikingly accurate – unsurprisingly, as Geoffrey of Monmouth, who apparently concocted the prophecies himself, was writing after the event.

As far as the dragons were concerned, Merlin revealed that the red dragon stood for the Celtic people (to this day it remains the Welsh national symbol) and the white for the Saxons. Like the dragons, the two peoples were

> "woe to you, Normandy, because the lion's brain shall be poured upon you, and he shall be banished with shattered limbs from his native soil."
>
> (MERLIN PROPHESYING THE DEATH OF HENRY I OF ENGLAND IN NORMANDY ON 1 DECEMBER 1135, AS RECORDED BY GEOFFREY OF MONMOUTH IN THE 1150S)

The sword in the stone

In modern times, Merlin's best-known prediction is probably the story of the sword in the stone: King Uther Pendragon's dying command that whoever could draw a blade magically embedded in an anvil placed on a boulder should be his heir as king of Britain. In the story, Merlin's pupil and protégé Arthur achieves the feat after many famous knights have failed, and so succeeds to the throne. Geoffrey of Monmouth, in fact, does not mention this story, which makes its first appearance in the work of Robert de Boron, a Burgundian poet writing half a century later. De Boron's poem *Merlin* also made another lasting contribution to the Arthurian legend: he introduced the Round Table, around which Arthur's knights could gather on an equal footing without having to worry about questions of precedence in the seating arrangements.

A *15th-century illustration from* St Alban's Chronicle *depicts Vortigern and the young Merlin watching the battle of the red and white dragons, representing Celts and Saxons respectively, as described in Geoffrey of Monmouth's* Historia.

Madman of the borders

Since the prophecies have largely been attributed to Geoffrey of Monmouth's imagination, Merlin's reputation as a seer has taken a battering. Yet there are indications that Geoffrey in fact drew on genuine ancient Celtic sources, raising the possibility that a real-life precursor of Merlin actually existed. The story of the fatherless child and the fighting dragons had, for example, appeared in an eighth-century history in which the boy's name was given as Ambrosius. His feat of prediction supposedly took place at a sixth-century Celtic court.

Geoffrey tapped a different tradition in a shorter work, the *Vita Merlini*, that he wrote a dozen years after the *Historia*. This 1,500-line verse biography of the seer describes a very different figure from the Arthurian Merlin. It tells of a sixth-century king and prophet from Dyfed in South Wales who fought in alliance with the King of Cumbria against a King of Scocia (Scotland). Maddened by grief following the death of his three brothers in battle, the king withdrew to the Caledonian Forest in the Scottish borders, occasionally re-emerging to utter prophecies that sometimes echo those in the *Historia*.

destined to fight each other; at first the Saxons would prevail, although later the Celts would rise again.

Geoffrey, however, did not stop writing prophecies when he reached his own time – he went on to put in Merlin's mouth genuine predictions for the centuries still to come. Most of these are too obscure to be easily interpreted. In later years, William Shakespeare poked fun at them in his play *Henry IV, Part I*, in which Hotspur sneers at "the dreamer Merlin and his prophecies".

The only "Merlin" prediction that can be verified with any certainty is one that foresees a time of Celtic resurgence – as with the dragons' story – when "the islands shall be called once more by the name of Brutus". The name

"Britain" did, of course, come back into use after the union of the English and Scottish crowns in 1603. Even so, Merlin's words hardly qualify as prophetic, because the forgers of the union between the kingdoms were aware of them when they chose the name. For, surprisingly, Merlin's enigmatic pronouncements, as described by Geoffrey, remained hugely influential for centuries to come. Many readers eagerly sought contemporary applications. James I, the first king of a united England and Scotland, echoed Geoffrey's vision in stating that "being King of the whole island he would be King of Britain, as Brutus and Arthur were who had the style, and were kings of the whole island".

merlin and stonehenge

In Geoffrey of Monmouth's *Historia*, Merlin is responsible for setting the great stone circle of Stonehenge on Salisbury Plain in southern England. Geoffrey's book describes how, after Vortigern's fall, the new ruler of Britain, Aurelius, determined to build a memorial for a group of nobles treacherously slain by Vortigern's Saxon ally, Hengist. However, as with Vortigern's fortress (see main text and picture below), there were construction problems that were only solved when Merlin was consulted. The wizard recommended transporting to the site a monumental complex already standing in Ireland – a feat he then accomplished by the use of magic. The result, according to Geoffrey, was the erection of the monument "known in the English language as Stonehenge" (see page 82).

This Merlin bears unmistakable resemblance to an actual Welsh bard known as Myrddin, whose writings Geoffrey was evidently familiar with. Surviving fragments of Myrddin's work include autobiographical poems in which he speaks of himself as an outlaw and madman, leading a solitary life in the Caledonian Forest following a battle.

The figure of the prophet driven mad by grief also crops up elsewhere in Welsh literature, and similarities in the names of associated characters indicate that the individual concerned is the same one as in the Myrddin poems. However, in some prose fragments, he is referred to as Laloecen or Lailoken. The most revealing of these texts is a life of St Kentigern, the patron saint of Glasgow. It describes how the saint met a naked madman in a wood who told him that he had lost his senses during a terrible battle fought near the River Liddell, close to the English–Scottish border. Subsequently this wild figure attached himself to the saint, sometimes interrupting his sermons with prophetic utterances. The madman was eventually reconciled to Christianity, but not before making a final prediction that he would die, uniquely, in three different ways at once. Unlikely though the prospect seemed, his words were borne out when he was stoned by some shepherds, slipped down a bank of the River Tweed and was then impaled on a sharp stake in the riverbed, thereby expiring simultaneously of battery, impalement and drowning.

Far from being the wizard of modern legend, the original Merlin may, then, have been a "wild man of the woods", naked and hairy. Nikolai Tolstoy, author of *The Quest for Merlin*, published in 1985, even claims to have found the spring, high up on the slopes of Hart Fell in the Scottish borders, where the seer lived.

As a real-life prophet, this Merlin certainly fits neatly into the larger history of the subject in one unfortunate respect: his clairvoyance apparently brought him little joy, and could not prevent him from meeting the miserable fate that is usually the destiny of prophets.

The remains of the Welsh fortress Dinas Emrys (in the left foreground), which is said to be the stronghold built by Vortigern where Merlin revealed the existence of the warring red and white dragons.

wizards and wise women

The success of Geoffrey of Monmouth's Merlin prophecies (see pages 106–9) set off an extraordinary vogue for the genre that stretched through the Middle Ages and on into the sixteenth and seventeenth centuries. The fashion was especially marked in Britain. Many of the predictions – and there were literally hundreds of them – in time developed a life of their own. They circulated by word of mouth, and were often attributed over the course of time to many different sources. By the seventeenth century, enterprising publishers were bringing out collections: *Sundry Strange Prophecies of Merlin, [the Venerable] Bede, [Thomas à] Becket, and Others* came out in 1652. Usually the auguries were couched in allegorical terms – following the fashion set by Geoffrey of Monmouth, they were peopled with white lions, dragons, eagles and wolves, and it was left to individual interpreters to determine the intended reference.

Dozens of now-obscure individuals, including Truswell, Otwell Binns and Old Harlock, were credited over the years with authorship of the predictions, but a few names still stand out from the crowd. One such was Thomas of Ercildoune – now Earlston, near Melrose in the Scottish borders – who is better remembered as Thomas the Rhymer.

Thomas actually existed; he was the author of an Arthurian verse romance, *Sir Tristram*. His prophecies were mostly concerned with Scottish history. One that seems to have helped spread his fame concerned the death of King Alexander III in 1286. Knowing of Thomas's reputation for second sight, a nobleman, Lord March, asked him for a forecast of what the next day might have in store. Thomas replied that "before the next day at noon, such a tempest would blow as Scotland had not felt for many years". The next day in fact dawned bright and clear, and Lord March was chaffing the prophet for his inaccuracy when a messenger arrived to say that the king – a long-lived monarch whose reign had been something of a golden age – had been killed in a riding accident. The king's horse had plunged off a cliff. "This is the tempest I foretold," claimed Thomas, "and so it shall prove for Scotland".

In time legends grew up around Thomas's name, crediting his clairvoyance to supernatural origins. A famous border ballad describes how he met the queen of Fairyland one day while walking on the Eildon Hills. She took him on horseback to her underground realm, where he remained, forbidden to talk, for seven years. When he was finally allowed to return home he was given the gift of always speaking the truth, whether about the past, the present or the future, which soon won him fame as a prophet. But he was always on parole to his fairy mistress, and one day she sent a hart to the streets of Earlston as a sign that Thomas should return to her dominion. He left instantly, and was never seen again by mortal eyes.

The "Marvellous Doctor"
Roger Bacon was a close contemporary of Thomas of Ercildoune: both men were born around 1220 and both

> "vessels may be made to move without oars or rowers, so that ships of great size could travel on the sea or rivers, steered by a single man, faster than if they were strongly manned."
>
> (Roger Bacon, foreseeing steamships 600 years before their invention)

The queen of the fairies — portrayed in this oil painting by the 19th-century Scottish artist Sir Joseph Noel Paton — is said to have whisked Thomas of Ercildoune away to her realm, where she bestowed upon him his famous prophetic powers.

lived to the 1290s. However, in other respects they could hardly have been more different. Bacon was a brilliant intellectual who studied at Oxford and Paris and turned his attention to many fields of learning: not just mathematics, astronomy and optics, but also alchemy and astrology, which, at the time, were still regarded as legitimate fields of study.

After teaching in Paris for some years, Bacon returned to Oxford in 1247 to devote himself to scientific enquiry. Becoming interested in the prophecies of Joachim of Fiore (see pages 32–5), he decided to join the Franciscan order, which had been set up some years

earlier under Joachite influence. It was an unfortunate move. Bacon was uncomfortable with the disciplines required within the order, which in turn regarded his intellectual speculations with growing suspicion. Eventually he was imprisoned at the monks' insistence for "suspected novelties" in his teaching. He died unfulfilled and embittered.

In contrast to Thomas's visions, Bacon's prophecies were much more in the mould of rational, though extraordinarily far-sighted, predictions. He worked with lenses and with gunpowder, and foresaw their future uses, respectively in telescopes and microscopes and in

This late 15th-century Florentine manuscript depicts Roger Bacon as a Franciscan monk in his study. Bacon, who was one of the great scholars of his time, lived to regret his decision to join the Franciscans, who condemned his predictions of future scientific progress as heretical.

cannons. He also speculated on the possibilities of human flight, proposing a hot-air balloon (to be made of thin copper sheet and propelled by "liquid fire") and envisioning a flying machine in which a man, "sitting at his ease and meditating on any subject, may beat the air with artificial wings". He foresaw machines that would climb walls – prototype elevators – and that would enable men "to walk on the bottom of the sea". Such novel

thinking, along with his alchemical and astrological studies, won him a lasting reputation for magical powers. By the time of the popular Elizabethan comedy *Friar Bacon and Friar Bungay*, written by Robert Greene in the 1590s, Bacon was seen as a fully-fledged wizard and was credited with the invention of a bronze head with the power of speech. It was an incongruous fate for an intellectual who in his day had won the title of *doctor mirabilis* – "Marvellous Doctor".

The Cheshire Idiot and Mother Shipton

Two humbler English prophets long remembered after their deaths were Robert Nixon and Ursula Southiel, who is known to this day under her married name of Mother Shipton. Nixon was by all accounts a village idiot – ugly, taciturn, lazy and gluttonous. Born in the county of Cheshire in 1467, he found work as a ploughboy and first attracted attention when he correctly predicted the death of his employer's prize ox. Word of Nixon's prophetic

> "I have seen things I cannot tell you, and which man never saw before."
>
> (Robert Nixon, the Cheshire Prophet, on emerging from a trance)

gifts reached the local great family, the Cholmondsleys, who tried in vain to educate him. He eventually returned to ploughing, but his work was occasionally interrupted by long periods of inactivity during which he apparently went into trances. On the basis of what he saw in his visions, he not only foretold local storms and floods, but also supposedly described major events of future European history, predicting both the English Civil War and the French Revolution.

One day in 1485 Nixon attracted attention by stopping work to indulge in a mock battle, shadow-boxing invisible opponents. As he did so, he shouted out the names "Richard" and "Henry" – the imaginary bout ended when "Henry" won. Two days later, messengers arrived to announce that the Battle of Bosworth Field had been fought at the time of Nixon's outburst. Henry VII's victory over Richard III had ended the Wars of the Roses and established the Tudor dynasty on England's throne.

As so often in the history of prophecy, the Cheshire Prophet's talents brought him fame but little joy. Word of his abilities reached King Henry, who summoned him to court and ordered a scribe to follow him around in case inspiration should strike. But Nixon's gluttony proved his undoing. He kept stealing food, and one day, when the king had left on a hunting expedition, an exasperated cook locked the prophet in a cellar and then forgot about

An untimely end

Like Roger Bacon, Michael Scot (ca. 1175–1230) was a brilliant intellectual who acquired a reputation as a wizard. Besides translating Aristotle, Scot studied in several countries and served as tutor to the brilliant, free-thinking Holy Roman Emperor, Frederick II. Scot also wrote several works on astrology, winning for himself a place in Dante's *Inferno* among the ranks of the sorcerers. Yet stories tell that his occult skills could not save him from an untimely end. Having foreseen that he would die from a blow to the head, he took to wearing an iron helmet at all times for protection. But one day, when attending church in the company of the emperor, he was forced to remove the helmet as a mark of respect. During the service a brick fell from the roof and killed Scot, just as he had predicted.

him. The king returned a couple of weeks later and asked after his charge, but it was too late to save Nixon – he had died of dehydration and starvation.

Mother Shipton's prophecies have remained in print, and the cave (see picture, below left) where she supposedly uttered them is still a tourist attraction. Her best-known prophecy was a prediction of the fate of Henry VIII's chief minister, Cardinal Wolsey. When he had fallen from favour with the king and was returning to his old position as Archbishop of York, Mother Shipton insisted that he would never reach the city. In fact he got within 7 miles (12 km) of it before being summoned back to face treason charges in London; he died on the way. However, as none of the predictions attributed to Mother Shipton were published until 180 years after her death, it is impossible to know now whether any were genuine. Most seem to have been made up after the event.

The famous Petrifying Well at Mother Shipton's Cave near Knaresborough in Yorkshire, northern England, has been drawing visitors to the site linked with the medieval seer for hundreds of years. Rich in lime, the cascading water in the cave turns the many everyday objects left there to stone.

the Templar's curse

One of the great orders of chivalry, the Knights Templars, was originally set up to perform a specific mission. The year was 1119, and Jerusalem had been conquered 20 years earlier in the course of the First Crusade. Pilgrims from all over Europe were eager to visit the Holy City, but they did so at considerable risk. The holy places were Christian strongholds in hostile territory, and many pilgrims did not survive the 30-mile (50-km) journey overland from the port of Jaffa. A French nobleman named Hugues de Payens proposed to found the Knights Templars to provide armed guards to police the route to Jerusalem. In 1128 a church council at Troyes in France approved the establishment of the order.

From the start, the Templars intended to be more than common soldiery, although they quickly established a reputation as fighting men. The knights saw their vocation as a religious one, and they aspired to the status of military monks. Like other monks, they took vows of poverty, chastity and obedience and were organized in a strict hierarchy under the leadership of a Grand Master. They themselves came from noble families, but they had a whole retinue of non-noble soldiers and servants to assist them and minister to their needs.

In the heyday of the crusading era, the Templars not only won many military honours, but also became rich. Huge donations poured into their coffers to help the knights fight the good fight. Before long they were also taking responsibility for other people's money – for in a time of general insecurity and unrest the Templars acted as bankers, holding funds securely in their heavily guarded fortresses.

Inevitably, the Templars' growing prosperity attracted envy, and at the same time the secrecy of their lives encouraged gossip. People took to wondering what strange rites might go on behind the high walls of the order's castles. As long as the knights continued to play a frontline role in the defence of the Holy Land, such criticisms were muted. However,

Jacques de Molay, the last Grand Master of the Knights Templars, said to have successfully cursed both King Philip the Fair of France and Pope Clement V at the time of his execution in 1314.

when the last Christian stronghold was abandoned in 1291, the Templars lost much of their prestige along with their original purpose.

Suddenly European rulers, who were running out of cash to fund their interminable wars, started listening to the tales that circulated about the Templars' supposed abuses. There were rumours of homosexual orgies in their all-male bastions – even hints of satanic rites brought back to Europe from the heathen lands.

In 1307 King Philip the Fair of France determined finally to put an end to the order. He seized their head-quarters in Paris, and commanded

> " … and he would have confessed that he had slain god himself if they had asked him that."
>
> (Contemporary chronicler on Jacques de Molay's confession, made under torture)

that every Templar should be arrested. He then bullied Pope Clement V, a Frenchman very much under the king's sway, into allowing him to put the knights on trial. Armed with papal authority, Philip proceeded to have the knights tortured in the most brutal ways. Subjected to the rack and the thumbscrew, to the wedge and slow fires, 36 of the detainees died painfully. Many others proved ready to confess to whatever charges were put before them: even improbable claims that they had practised blasphemy by urinating on the cross, or had worshipped the devil in the form of a black cat that they kissed under the tail.

Armed with these lurid confessions, Philip sent 54 individuals to be burned at the stake, and then, in 1312, had the order itself dissolved. Officially, its remaining assets were transferred to the Knights Hospitallers, a sister order, although in practice much of the Templars' wealth ended up in the royal treasury.

The fate of the Grand Master
Jacques de Molay, the last Grand Master of the Knights Templars, played a central part in the tragedy.

Like many of his brethren, he confessed under torture and Philip decided to make a spectacle of him. In March 1314 de Molay was led out, with his second-in-command, to the square in front of Notre Dame cathedral in Paris. The Grand Master had been ordered to publicly acknowledge his guilt before being taken off to a lifetime of imprisonment. But de Molay refused to play the part assigned to him. Presented with an audience, he recanted the confession that had been extorted from him and proclaimed his innocence.

Infuriated, Philip gave orders that both men should be burned alive in the very same spot the following day. As the flames grew, de Molay again protested his innocence and then reportedly called down a curse on his persecutors: both King Philip and Pope Clement, he cried, would themselves be dead within the year.

If de Molay did indeed utter that prediction, it was quickly fulfilled. Clement – in his mid 50s at the time – was dead within the month, and the 46-year-old King Philip followed him to the grave the next November. Philip supposedly died from a stroke, but there were plenty of people ready to say at the time that he had in fact been struck down by God's wrath, just as the Templars' dying Grand Master had predicted.

An illustration from the 14th-century manuscript The Chronicle of France *depicts Jacques de Molay and his deputy being burned alive at the stake.*

Nostradamus and the *centuries*

Nostradamus is probably the most famous secular prophet of all time, but his life story has become so encrusted with legend that it is difficult to separate fact from fiction in the published accounts. However, the basic outline of his biography is generally agreed. He was born in St-Rémy-de-Provence in southern France in 1503 and died in Salon, about 19 miles (30 km) away, in 1566. Nostradamus travelled widely in France and Italy, but regularly returned to his home region of Provence and eventually settled there. Also uncontroversial is the fact that his reputation as a prophet was firmly established in his own lifetime. In the last 20 years of his life he attracted disciples to Salon, won the attention of the French court, gained wealth and honours in his old age, and even acquired a measure of international fame.

Christened Michel de Nostredame – Nostradamus is a Latinization – the future seer was born into a family of Jewish background that had converted to Catholicism sometime before his birth. His grandfather was a grain merchant who also acted as a notary. He was apparently a man of learning, and he is said to have given the young Nostradamus a solid educational grounding, not just in the classics and mathematics but also in astronomy.

As a young man Nostradamus first studied at Avignon, and then transferred to Montpellier, famous for its faculty of medicine, where he qualified as a doctor in 1529. For the next two decades he earned his living as a travelling physician, winning a reputation for his unconventional and humane methods: he refused to bleed his patients, although bleeding was then standard treatment for many ailments, and preferred ligatures to cauterization as a way of staunching the flow of blood from wounds. His professional career was played out against a background of plague, which was then endemic in

By the time of his death, Nostradamus was not only famous but also wealthy. In his will he left a legacy of over 3,400 crowns – a fortune at the time for a provincial doctor. A detail from a wall mural in modern St Rémy.

southern France, and which carried away his first wife – described as a girl "of high estate, very beautiful and admirable" – and their two small children.

A gift for prophecy

If the stories are to be believed, in the course of his wanderings Nostradamus gradually built up a reputation for inexplicable foresight. On one occasion, in Italy, he knelt down before a young monk who passed him in the street, addressing him as "Your Holiness". The young man was Felice Peretti, a one-time swineherd who became Pope Sixtus V in 1585, 19 years after Nostradamus's death. Another story tells how once, when Nostradamus was a dinner guest, a host tried to disprove his abilities by asking him to predict the fate of two pigs, one black and one white. Nostradamus replied that they would eat the black pig, while a wolf would devour the white one. The host then gave secret instructions to his cook to prepare the white pig for dinner, and when the meal was served confronted his guest with the edible evidence of his error. But Nostradamus stuck to his guns. Eventually the cook was summoned, and confounded his employer by confessing that it was indeed the black pig that they had eaten; he had been preparing to cook the white one when a wolf cub that was being held on the estate had

> "I emptied my soul, brain and heart of all care and attained a state of tranquillity and stillness of mind which are prerequisites for predicting by means of the brass tripod." (NOSTRADAMUS, EPISTLE TO HENRY II)

broken into the kitchen and made off with it.

Nostradamus started building a serious reputation as a prophet only after settling down in Salon in 1547. From 1550 on he started publishing annual almanacs forecasting the events of the year ahead. Then in 1555 he published the first edition of the *Centuries*, the work for which he is remembered today. The title did not refer to future ages; it was used because Nostradamus chose to group his prophecies, written in four-line rhyming verses, in groups of 100. The first edition included three centuries and part of a fourth – a total of 353 verses. A second edition, published three years later, raised the

NOSTRADAMUS'S METHODS

The first two verses of the first of the *Centuries* are unlike anything that follows. In them Nostradamus makes no predictions, but instead paints an oblique, allusive picture of his own working methods. The first reads: "*Etant assis de nuit secret étude/Seul reposé sur la selle aérienne; /Flambe exigué sortant de solitude/Fait prospérer qui n'est à croire vain*". ("Seated by night in secret study/Alone resting on the bronze tripod/A thin flame coming out of solitude/Prospers what is not believed in vain.") The second continues the theme: "*La verge en main mise au milieu des branches/De l'onde il mouille & les limbes & les pieds/Un* peur & voix frémissant par les manches:/Splendeur divine. Le divin près s'assied". ("The wand in hand set in the middle of the branches/With water he sprinkles the hem of his garment and his feet/Fear and a voice; trembling in his robes:/Divine splendour. The god sits down close by.") Taken together, the two verses suggest an invocation summoning a divine being. Scholars have compared the method to that employed by the fourth-century Neoplatonist Iamblichus, whose work *De Mysteriis Egyptorum* (Concerning the Mysteries of Egypt) had been reprinted in Lyons in 1547.

When Henry II of France died as the result of an injury sustained at a tournament in a manner seemingly described in one of the quatrains, there were anti-Nostradamus riots in Paris. Citizens blamed the seer for the death they thought he had predicted.

number to 642, while a third, printed posthumously in 1568, brought the total to 942. For unexplained reasons the seventh century remained incomplete.

Possibly because Nostradamus's reputation had already begun to spread, the *Centuries* proved an instant success. Within a year of its first publication, Nostradamus had been summoned to court to meet King Henry II and his celebrated wife, Catherine de Medici. Catherine asked the Provençal prophet to prepare horoscopes for her four children, and on a royal tour through the provinces in 1564 she even went to visit him in Salon.

Royal favour ensured that Nostradamus's reputation spread widely, even beyond France's borders. When Queen Elizabeth I ascended the English throne in 1559, just four years after the publication of the first edition of the *Centuries*, all England was said to be caught up in contemplating the "blind, enigmatical and devilish prophecies of that heaven-gazer Nostradamus".

The appeal of ambiguity

There are good reasons why Nostradamus's prophecies continue to exert such a fascination almost half a millennium after his death.

Few seers have left so solid a body of work: 942 separate predictions, for all of which the authorship is reasonably certain. The predictions' appeal does not appear to be diminished by the enticingly confused state in which they are presented. Only a handful mention a specific date, although Nostradamus claimed that he could, if he had so wished, have put dates to all of them. (He said he feared to do so, however, lest he be accused of witchcraft.) The lack of any fixed chronology makes the prophecies open to endless re-interpretations — whenever a major event happens anywhere in the world, there are 900 or so possible Nostradamus quatrains to apply to it.

The uncertainty stretches to the language Nostradamus chose to use. His gnomic verses are small masterpieces of ambiguity. Even the grammar and punctuation are rarely clear. The language itself is allusive and obscure, borrowing or inventing

"He will make his entrance, wicked, bad, ill-famed/Tyrannizing over Mesopotamia/All friends made of an adulterous spirit/The land horrible, black of aspect."

(NOSTRADAMUS PROPHECY SOMETIMES INTERPRETED AS PREDICTING SADDAM HUSSEIN'S ROLE IN THE GULF WAR)

words derived from Greek, Latin, Hebrew and other languages alongside Nostradamus's native French. The results are predictions that, in some respects, resemble clues for an extraordinarily difficult crossword puzzle. Some people have spent half a lifetime combing the quatrains for anagrams and coded meanings, but so far no-one has produced a consistently satisfactory interpretation of them.

Kings and tragedies

In spite of the ambiguity of a lot of his work, many of Nostradamus's verses are tantalizingly evocative of events that often long postdated them: none more so, perhaps, than the quatrain that first established his reputation. This stated that: "The young lion will overcome the old/ On the field of battle in single combat/He will put out his eyes in a golden cage/Two wounds one, then to die a cruel death". The prophet's contemporaries had no hesitation in applying the verses to a tragedy that occurred in 1559, four years after the quatrain was published. The French king Henry II took part in a tournament staged to celebrate two royal weddings. His younger opponent's lance accidentally penetrated the monarch's visor – the "golden cage" of the prophecy – piercing him behind the eye. The king died in great pain a week later.

Other Nostradamus prophecies have been applied rather less convincingly to some of the great events of later European history. "The fortress near the Thames will fall/ When the king is locked inside/He will be seen in his shirt near the bridge/One facing death, then locked inside the fort", for example, is often seen as predicting the execution of Charles I of England, famously beheaded in his shirt-sleeves. However, no fortress fell, and Westminster Bridge – the nearest to the place of execution – was not built until many years later, further reducing the forecast's accuracy.

A few prophecies seem to have a more apt application. Quatrain 38 of the fifth century states: "He who will come to the throne on the death of the great monarch/Will lead an illicit and sensual life/Through

Nostradamus's quatrain "The blood of the just will be spilled at London/Burned by the fire of twenty three the sixes/The ancient lady will topple from a high place/Many of the same sect will be killed" is usually taken to refer to the Great Fire of London of 1666. Dutch School painting of the event, 17th century.

in overseas exploration, this is a remarkable example of foresight. The timespan also fits well – the first successful British colonies were established in the early seventeenth century, and most of those that remained were granted independence in the mid-twentieth century.

Nostradamus and Napoleon

In the first of the ten centuries, Nostradamus also seems to predict the rule of Napoleon. One verse proclaims: "An Emperor will be born near Italy/Who will cost the Empire dear./People will say when they see his supporters/That he has turned out not so much a prince as a butcher." Napoleon was born on the island of Corsica, less than 60 miles (100 km) from the Italian coast. The disenchanted description of the emperor's subsequent career would be natural enough for someone viewing Napoleon's revolutionary sympathies from a sixteenth-century perspective.

The end of Napoleon's career is perhaps hinted at in another quatrain that reads: "The great empire will soon be transformed/Into a small place that will soon start

insouciance he will make concessions to everyone/So that finally the Salic law will be needed." This verse applies neatly to the heir to the Sun King Louis XIV, Louis XV. The latter's pleasure-loving and indecisive reign paved the way for the French Revolution. The Salic law prevented women from taking the throne; the reference here would seem to be to the excessive influence of the king's mistresses, notably Madame de Pompadour.

The British Empire's rise and fall

The last prophecy in the *Centuries* is one of the most impressive of all, apparently predicting with startling accuracy the birth and decline of the British Empire. It reads: "The great empire will be [created] by England/Omnipotent for more than 300 years:/Great forces moving by land and sea,/The Portuguese will not be happy." Written at a time when England had no colonies and when Portuguese mariners had a clear lead

> "The sudden death of the first person/ will have changed and set another to rule/sooner or later come so high at such a young age/That by land and sea all had to fear him."
>
> (Nostradamus prophecy sometimes interpreted as referring to the Kennedy assassination)

to grow;/A tiny place in a minute county/In the midst of which he will come to lay down his sceptre." Here the obvious fit is with Napoleon's exile, first to the island of Elba and then to St Helena in the South Atlantic Ocean. Elba fits the second line, in that Napoleon escaped from it to regain control of France. However, St Helena, as an English possession, would be more appropriate for line three: Nostradamus here chose the word *comté*, used in French to refer to English counties.

The World Trade Center attack

On more recent events, Nostradamus proves as evocative and ambiguous as ever. Interest in his work surged in the wake of the terrorist attack on New York's World Trade Center on 11 September 2001. Garbled versions of Nostradamus prophecies appeared on the internet within hours of the tragic events. Most drew on two separate prophecies, sometimes disingenuously combined to increase their relevance.

One is dated, but is 26 months out. It reads: "In the year 1999 and seven months/From the sky will come a great King of terror/To revive the great king of the Angolmois/ Before and after, Mars will happily reign." Here the first, second and last line all seem appropriate, if the "King of terror" is taken to describe Osama bin Laden and Mars is viewed in his classical role as god of war.

The third line, however, contains serious difficulties. The obvious reference is to the city of Angoulême in France. In that case, the person referred to would most likely have been Francis I, who ruled France for much of Nostradamus's life. Francis had been Duke of Angoulême before his accession, and would seem to fit the words well, but he has no conceivable connection with the events of 11 September. However, some commentators interpret the word as a near-anagram for *Mongolois*, or "Mongols", suggesting an attempt to revive an Eastern empire reminiscent of Genghis Khan's – an interpretation that would be more appropriate, if rather strained.

The other prophecy states: "At 45 degrees the sky will burn/Fire approaches the great new city/In an instant great scattered flames will leap up/When someone will want to test the Normans." New York – the "great new city" – actually lies at a latitude of between 40 and 41 degrees north. Here, the relevance of the final line depends on taking "Normans" not to refer to inhabitants of Normandy, but in the less obvious sense of "Northmen". Between them, the two verses are classic Nostradamus – the words are teasingly suggestive, but almost impossible to pin down to a single clear meaning.

An unfulfilled prophecy for New York?

Another of Nostradamus's verses is often taken to refer to New York. It runs: "The world's garden near the new city/In the road of the hollow mountains/Will be taken up and plunged in the basin/Forced to drink sulfurous poisoned waters". As always with Nostradamus, the sense is ambiguous, but the words seem to hint at some still-to-come environmental disaster. Ingenious commentators have even claimed that "hollow mountains" could be the sixteenth-century seer's way of describing skyscrapers.

The cazotte prophecy

One evening early in 1787 or 1788 – accounts differ on the date – a glittering assembly attended a society dinner in Paris. About 60 people were present, among them many members of the French capital's intellectual aristocracy, including the writer Jacques Cazotte. Unlike most of the other guests, Cazotte was not a devotee of the Cult of Reason that was Enlightenment France's conventional orthodoxy. Instead, he flirted with Christian Neoplatonism, and had a minor reputation for foretelling future events.

Conversation after dinner turned on the Age of Reason, the dawn of which most intellectuals were expecting imminently. Breaking into the discussion,

Cazotte assured the guests that a revolution was indeed coming, but it would be very different from the triumph of rationalism they all expected. He insisted that the revolution would have terrible consequences for many of the individuals present. For example, he predicted that the author Sebastian-Roch Chamfort would slash his wrists in despair and die some months later. Chrétien de Malesherbes (an aristocrat and government-appointed supervisor of publishing) and the astronomer Jean Sylvain Bailly would both perish on the scaffold, as would the poet Jean-Antoine Roucher. When Jean de la Harpe, a dramatist and critic who was also present, sought to know what was in store for him, Cazotte foresaw a twist of

Cazotte's prediction of hope and rational behaviour giving way to terror proved all too accurate. Death was to stalk even the highest in the land. A 19th-century engraving of Louis XVI's execution.

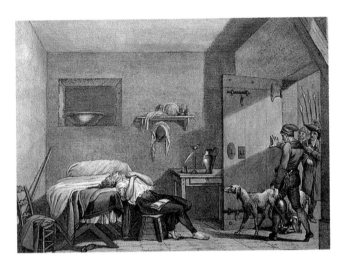

A coloured print depicts the suicide of the brilliant philosopher the Marquis de Condorcet on 28 March 1794. Just as Cazotte had foretold, Condorcet swallowed poison in his prison cell.

fate that seemed quite as unlikely as any so far: de la Harpe, a famous atheist, would become a Christian.

The Duchesse de Gramont commented that at least the ladies present might escape such horrors. But Cazotte replied that she would not be spared, and nor would the greatest in the land – a clear reference to Queen Marie Antoinette and her consort, Louis XVI. When asked of

his own fate, Cazotte responded by telling a story from the Jewish historian Josephus of a man who foresaw the fall of Jerusalem and was himself killed when it duly came to pass (see pages 62–3).

Cazotte's extraordinary words left a strong enough impression on the guests for one at least, Jean de la Harpe, to note the details down. And, if the account that was eventually published in his name can be believed, they proved extraordinarily prescient. The fates that Cazotte had foreseen for individual guests nearly all came to pass over the next seven years as the intellectuals who initially welcomed the Revolution were swept away in the ensuing reign of terror. Even the details proved correct: Chamfort's initial attempt to end his life by cutting his wrists failed, and he subsequently died as a result of incompetent medical treatment. Cazotte, having become involved in an unsuccessful plot to free the king, met his own fate courageously on the guillotine. As for de la Harpe himself, he underwent conversion while in jail and eventually died in a monastery.

There seems little doubt that, in general outline, the Cazotte prophecy was uttered as de la Harpe described – in later years, several eye-witnesses who had been at the dinner came forward to vouch for the accuracy of his account. It also seems clear that de la Harpe did indeed put his notes in writing soon afterwards, before the events foretold by Cazotte took place. A letter dated January 1789 has been found in which the writer speaks of reading "the famous prophecy of M. Cazotte". That implies that the text circulated privately, for the published version did not appear until 1806. A suspicion therefore lingers that the accuracy of the surviving account may have been embellished in hindsight. Even so, Cazotte's extraordinary words clearly had a profound effect on his audience, both at the time and even more so in the light of subsequent events.

pRophecy and the Revolution

One of Nostradamus's quatrains contains another frequently quoted prediction about the French Revolution:

Le règne pris le Roi conjurera,
La dame prise à mort jurés de sort:
La vie à Reine fils on déniera,
Et la pellix au fort de la consort.

The words translate as: "The kingdom taken the king will conspire,/The lady taken to death sworn by lot:/Life to Queen son will be denied,/And the mistress at the fortress of the wife." Those who view the lines as prophetic point out that, after his fall, King Louis XVI was charged with conspiracy, and that the jurors who condemned his wife to death were, unusually, chosen by lot. Taken captive, the queen's son, the Dauphin, disappeared, presumed dead. The final line is generally interpreted as referring to Madame du Barry, mistress of the king's grandfather Louis XV, who also lost her life.

"second sight" in the scottish Highlands

One of the strongest local prophetic traditions is the second sight documented in the Scottish Highlands from at least the seventeenth century on. According to one nineteenth-century authority on the region, the existence of one or more individuals with clairvoyant powers was "a fact indisputable in almost every one of the more rural communities". The writer Samuel Johnson, investigating the phenomenon on his tour of the Western Isles of Scotland in 1773, reported that "the islanders of all degrees, whether of rank or understanding, universally admit it, except the ministers, who universally deny it". Johnson himself was inclined to believe the stories.

Of all the thousands of individuals credited with clairvoyant powers, none is better remembered than Coinneach Oddhar, known as the Brahan Seer. Born on the island of Lewis in the Outer Hebrides early in the seventeenth century, Oddhar spent most of his life as a farmhand near Brahan Castle at the head of the Cromarty Firth, about 9 miles (15 km) northeast of Inverness. Tradition has it that he acquired his powers along with a magic stone; some stories say that the stone was given to his mother by a spirit, others that the seer found it for himself after dozing off on a fairy mound.

Like most Highlanders with the "gift", Oddhar took little pleasure in his abilities and made no attempt to exploit his talent. Visions of the future apparently came upon him without warning.

Highland tradition credits several dozen prophecies to the Brahan Seer. Unfortunately, as none were written down in his lifetime, it is impossible now to say which may have been added by hearsay. If the stories can be believed, some of Oddhar's previsions were remarkably accurate. His description of seeing the hills of the county of Ross strewn with ribbons is generally taken as a vision of the roads that eventually crisscrossed them. On one occasion, when crossing the future battlefield of Culloden, where the remnants of Bonnie Prince Charlie's Highland army were to be slaughtered by English redcoats in 1746, Oddhar stopped and shuddered, remarking that many heads would be lopped off there one day.

Like other prophets before him, Oddhar came to a bad end because of his gifts. Having offended the Countess of Seaforth with one of his exhibitions of clairvoyance, he was sentenced to death. However, before his execution he supposedly took his revenge by foretelling in great detail the final demise of the Seaforth family — a prediction that was realized to the letter almost two centuries later.

Some of Oddhar's predictions that have not yet been fulfilled are equally intriguing. One amounted to nothing

> "The day will come when long strings of carriages without horses shall run between Dingwall and Inverness and, more wonderfully still, between Dingwall and the Isle of Skye."
>
> (ONE OF THE BRAHAN SEER'S PROPHECIES, SUPPOSEDLY FORESEEING THE BUILDING OF RAILWAYS ACROSS THE SCOTTISH HIGHLANDS)

The Brahan Seer foresaw a day when "full-rigged ships will sail east and west by the back of Tomnahurich Hill", a spot near Inverness — 150 years after his death the Caledonian Canal, seen here, crossed the spot.

less than a preview of the whole future of the Highlands. Oddhar foresaw a time when sheep would replace humans over much of the region, only to disappear eventually in their turn. The land would then pass from the hands of its former owners to "merchant proprietors", and would next become a vast deer park, its people long gone to unknown islands. But that time too would come to an end; eventually the deer and other wildlife would be exterminated by a terrible black rain, and the people would eventually return again.

A nuclear disaster to come?

Much of this vision already rings true. The Highland Clearances of the eighteenth century saw a large part of the population driven out to make room for sheep, and many displaced Highlanders did indeed emigrate. Eventually, sheep farming became unprofitable, and the great estates were sold as bases for deer-stalking and shooting.

The final part of the prophecy has yet to come to pass, but another of the seer's unfulfilled predictions contains a hint as to how it might occur. Oddhar spoke of the day when a hornless dun cow would rise from the waters of the Minch — the strait between the Hebrides and mainland Scotland — and with its bellowing would knock down the six chimneys of Gairloch House in Wester Ross. In recent times nuclear submarines have been stationed around Scotland's coasts, and some people are tempted to see in the seer's words the prophecy of a nuclear accident yet to happen.

The stone that moved

One prediction ascribed by some authorities to the Brahan Seer was spectacularly fulfilled late in the eighteenth century. It concerned the Stone of Petty, an 8-ton boulder located near the coast about 6 miles (10 km) east of Inverness. A time would come, according to the prediction, when the stone would be moved from its existing position — then about 820 feet (250 m) inland — to a similar distance out to sea. The predicted event came to pass on 20 February 1799, during a night of hurricane-force winds. No-one saw the stone move, and how it was shifted remains a mystery to this day.

the woman clothed with the sun

The year 1792 was a difficult one in Britain: across the English Channel, the French Revolution had not brought the hoped-for Age of Reason; instead, it was degenerating into the horrors of the Terror (see pages 122–3). All the accepted norms of life seemed under threat, and there was a growing sense that war with France was inevitable.

In that year, a 42-year-old domestic servant in the English city of Exeter started having visions. The unmarried daughter of a hard-up farmer, Joanna Southcott had had little education and previously had lived an unremarkable life. However, her dreams now became ominous and pregnant with meaning. "One night I dreamt I saw some men in the air who pitched with their horses upon the earth," she wrote. "The horses fought furious, and the men fought furious, and so frightened me that I awoke and thought the French would land."

Over the ensuing years Southcott had many more visions, and gradually built up a local reputation as a seer; she was said to have predicted bad harvests for 1799 and 1800 and to have correctly foreseen the demise of a bishop of Exeter. In her own view she was a new biblical prophet, receiving messages from a guiding light she called simply "the Spirit". Reading the Bible, she identified herself with the Woman Clothed with the Sun described in the Revelation

A contemporary print by Isaac Cruikshank shows the prophetess Joanna Southcott attacking the bishops. In fact, although the bishops consistently refused to endorse her revelations, Southcott never ceased to seek their approval.

> "This is a new thing amongst mankind, for a woman to be the greatest prophet that ever came into the world."
>
> (JOANNA SOUTHCOTT, DESCRIBING HER OWN MISSION)

12, the enemy of Satan whose coming heralded war in Heaven.

Southcott's followers
In 1801 Southcott published a pamphlet of her prophecies at her own expense. Her writings soon started to attract a national following. Wealthy supporters brought her to London in the following year, and rented a chapel from which she could spread her message. Those who attended were given signed papers that announced them to be among the elect. When a rumour spread that the "sealed", as holders of the letters became known, would have an improved chance of survival if Napoleon's revolutionary forces invaded England as was imminently feared, a black market grew up for the sale of the documents.

Throughout the period of the Napoleonic Wars, Southcott expanded her following, mostly among the poorer classes, although she also attracted some wealthy, educated backers. Before long there were Southcottian groups scattered across England, eagerly devouring the 60-plus books and pamphlets she produced apparently under the inspiration of "the Spirit". These insistently proclaimed the imminent coming of a new age: "We believe that there will be a New Heaven, as declared by the Spirit, and a New Earth, wherein dwelleth Righteousness."

However, by 1814, Napoleon's armies had been almost overcome and Southcott's support was starting to flag. It was then that she announced her greatest coup. At the age of 64, she, like the Woman Clothed with the Sun, was to give birth. The son she would bear, who was to be named Shiloh, would be a new messiah – one who would rule all nations with a rod of iron.

News of the forthcoming virgin birth caught the public imagination, and as the expected time of delivery approached huge crowds gathered nightly in the street outside the house where Southcott lay. She showed all the signs of pregnancy, and 17 of the 21 doctors consulted were said to have confirmed that she was indeed with child. Yet no baby appeared; instead, Southcott's own health began to deteriorate. Eventually, two months after the expected birth date, she breathed her last. A subsequent autopsy revealed no obvious signs of disease. It may be that she simply lost faith in her own mission, and with it the will to live.

Public interest in Southcott's revelations faded rapidly after her death, but a hard core of believers kept the faith. There were still a few dozen Southcottian groups active in the mid-1800s. Even into the twentieth century some individuals refused to believe that Southcott had really died; rather, they insisted, she had been spirited away into the wilderness for her own protection, like her model in the Revelation, "to be nourished for a time, and times ... from the face of the serpent".

A Disappointing Legacy

Joanna Southcott's principal legacy was a sealed box, said to contain prophecies of vital importance to the future of England, which was only to be opened in the presence of 24 bishops. The bishops, however, refused to comply, and eventually it was left to Britain's best-known ghosthunter, Harry Price, to open what was said to be the genuine box at Westminster Hall in London in June 1927. All the box was found to contain was a few pamphlets on prophecy, some coins and other oddments, and a novel called *The Surprises of Love* by John Cleland, author of *Fanny Hill*.

The sleeping prophet

One well-publicized seer whose reputation has suffered something of a setback recently is Edgar Cayce. Known primarily as a healer until his death in 1945, Cayce's reputation as a clairvoyant was boosted by the appearance of a posthumous biography, *The Sleeping Prophet*, published in 1967. The title derived from Cayce's habit of uttering predictions, along with medical advice, while in a trance state.

Cayce was born in 1877 on a farm near Hopkinsville in Kentucky. When he was seven or eight years old, sitting in a forest glade, he saw a bright light and heard a voice asking, as in a fairy tale, what talents he would like to possess. He requested the gift of healing, and thereafter supposedly had abnormal therapeutic powers.

By all accounts Cayce was a dedicated healer who did much good to those he treated. His record as a prophet, however, now looks less impressive. In his lifetime Cayce was known as the man who predicted the 1929 Wall Street Crash and the Second World War, although his actual words were always rather more vague than that statement implies. In 1929, six months before Black Thursday, Cayce told a stock-broker to sell his stocks because a financial collapse was coming – a prescient view, but there were other voices raised at the time to say that the market was looking overvalued. Similarly, shortly before the Second World War broke out Cayce warned army reservists to expect to be called up – not entirely unexpected advice, given the global political instability at the time.

Jess Stearn's *The Sleeping Prophet* chose to focus on a number of grandiose geophysical warnings Cayce outlined in trances in the mid-1930s. These indicated that the Earth was going to experience a sequence of catastrophic geological events between 1958 and 1998. The

Some of Edgar Cayce's contemporaries believed that he had foreseen the Wall Street Crash. Here, stunned investors gather in New York's financial district in October 1929.

globe's polar axis would move, and the ensuing tectonic shifts would cause land movements on a gigantic scale. San Francisco would be destroyed, California would slip into the ocean, and much of northern Europe and Japan would go the same way. New York too would eventually be destroyed; Cayce had a vision of himself returning to Earth in 2100 and landing amid the rubble of what had once been Manhattan.

Cayce was obviously fascinated by the notion of large-scale tectonic movement. Alfred Wegener had published his theories of continental drift in 1915, and the concept received increasing press coverage in the 1920s. Some of these ideas seem to have affected Cayce deeply, not only shaping his view of the planet's future, but also of its past. He became convinced that Atlantis — which in his view lay somewhere off the eastern coast of the USA — would

> "The earth will be broken up in the western portion of America. The greater portion of Japan must go into the sea. The upper portion of Europe will be changed in the twinkling of an eye. Land will appear off the east coast of America."
>
> (Edgar Cayce's unfulfilled trance predictions of major tectonic movements, made in January 1934)

rise again; he expected its western portion to surface near the Bahamas in the late 1960s. He also maintained that the lost continent had supported a great, technologically advanced civilization sometime before 10,000BCE, the records of which would be found in a secret chamber beneath the left paw of the Sphinx at Giza in Egypt between 1996 and 1998. Needless to say, none of

these events has actually occurred. Neither, fortunately, has another prediction, foreseeing the outbreak of a third world war in 1999 and the end of civilization as we know it.

Cayce may have had an unusual talent for entering trance states almost at will, but on the evidence of his published predictions, his subconscious vision had no reliable direct line to the future.

The poughkeepsie seer

Another American prophet whose reputation has faded with the years is Andrew Jackson Davis, the "Poughkeepsie Seer". Like Edgar Cayce, Davis had a vision as a child that started him on his prophetic career, and he also went into hypnotic trances to diagnose and cure ailments. He too claimed to have the gift of foresight in his trances, and some of his visions were subsequently recorded in books, notably *The Penetralia*, published in 1856. His imaginings were very much those of the early machine age: horseless carriages, prefabricated buildings, phonetic spelling, and a device that would print a person's ideas as readily as a piano broadcast tunes — not a bad advance description of computers. But Davis also had serious misses — he thought advanced life-forms would be found on Mars, Jupiter and Saturn — and today his works are little read.

the Hitler prophecies

Dramatic times often spawn prophets, and the Nazi era in Germany was no exception. Even in the years before Adolf Hitler came to power, life was far from stable for the German people – the aftermath of defeat in the First World War and the catastrophic inflation of 1922–1923 left them restless and uncertain about the future. One symptom of this general insecurity was a rise in the popularity of astrology, which had a greater following in Germany in the 1920s than anywhere else in Europe. Entrepreneurs such as the theosophist Hugo Vollrath, who organized congresses, set up publishing imprints and produced magazines, found a ready audience for their enterprises.

Another beneficiary of the boom was Elsbeth Ebertin, a graphologist and astrologer who published an annual almanac of predictions from 1917 on. In 1923 a female member of the infant National Socialist German Workers', or Nazi, Party, sent Ebertin details of Hitler's birth date, seeking to know what fate had in store for him. Without mentioning Hitler by name, Ebertin took up the subject in that year's almanac, which appeared late in July. She wrote: "A man of action born on April 20, 1889 [Hitler's birthday] … may expose himself to personal danger by excessively rash action and could very likely trigger an uncomfortable crisis. His constellations show that this man is to be taken very seriously indeed; he

Adolf Hitler (left), Field Marshal Hermann Goering (centre) and Nazi propaganda chief Joseph Goebbels (right) salute while crowds in Berlin sing the German national anthem in August 1943.

An artist's impression of the fire that swept through Berlin's parliament building, the Reichstag, on 27 February 1933. The astrologer Erik Hanussen, who had publicly predicted the fire the previous day, was to pay for the announcement with his life.

is destined to play a Führer role in future battles." That November, Hitler helped organize the abortive Munich putsch that led to his arrest and imprisonment. As for the rest of Ebertin's prediction, history bears witness.

Hitler himself was reportedly shown the horoscope and dismissed it curtly, saying, "Whatever have women and the stars got to do with me?" Contrary to rumour, he was never interested in or impressed by clairvoyants of any description, but others in the Nazi movement were more receptive. In particular, Heinrich Himmler, head of the Office for State Security, or SS, was fascinated by astrology, as was Hitler's deputy Rudolf Hess.

Hanussen's "predictions"

Others in the Party were prepared to make use of predictions to serve their own purposes. Both believers and opportunists played a part in the Hanussen affair, a murky episode that coincided with the Nazi Party's assumption of power in Germany in early 1933. Erik Jan Hanussen was a stage hypnotist and clairvoyant with a considerable reputation in Germany at the time. He also published a popular astrological weekly and gave private consultations to clients; he is even said to have employed bugging as a way of boosting the accuracy of his forecasts.

> " ... this man is to be taken very seriously indeed; he is destined to play a Führer role in future battles ... "
>
> (ELSBETH EBERTIN READING HITLER'S HOROSCOPE IN JULY 1923)

Despite the fact that he was part Jewish, Hanussen had contacts among the Nazis, and reportedly even gave Hitler lessons in public speaking. However, he also had enemies in the movement – the secret police, or Gestapo, was aware of his Jewish background.

When Hanussen cast Hitler's horoscope in January 1933, and correctly predicted that the latter would take power in Germany on the 30th of the month, voices were raised to say that the astrologer must have had inside information. The same claim came back to haunt Hanussen the following month, when he made an even more startling public revelation. On 26 February he was quoted in the press as saying, "I see a blood-curdling crime committed by the Communists. I see blazing flames. I see a terrible firebrand that lights up the world". The following evening, the prediction was spectacularly realized in the Reichstag fire. The Nazis did indeed blame the Communists for the burning down of Berlin's parliament building, although in fact there is

little doubt that the fire was started on the Nazis' own orders as a pretext for a purge of left-wingers.

How Hanussen came up with his prediction remains a mystery. According to some accounts, the prophecy was actually made by one of his associates, a medium named Marie Paudler, in the course of a séance. Others suspect that Hanussen had advance knowledge of the Nazis' planned act of sabotage through his contacts in the movement. Either way, there were evidently elements in the Party who were furious at having news of the fire broadcast so ostentatiously in advance. Some days later, Hanussen was intercepted on the way to a performance and was hustled into his own car. His bullet-ridden body was later found in a wood on the outskirts of Berlin.

Astrology and the Nazi Party

Karl Ernst Krafft was another clairvoyant on the fringes of the Nazi regime. A Swiss of German extraction, Krafft was a clever but eccentric youth who threw himself into abstruse attempts to prove the scientific validity of astrology through statistical analysis. Failing to win academic support for his projects, he drifted through a succession of jobs. In 1938 he moved to Germany, where he quickly decided to throw in his lot with the Nazis.

By following up a contact made through his astrological studies, Krafft managed to obtain freelance work with the SS. On 2 November 1939, a few months into his new posting, Krafft sent a startling report to Himmler's office. Hitler's horoscope, he claimed, indicated that enemies using explosives might endanger the Führer's life between the 7th and 10th of that month. As it turned out, Hitler escaped an assassination attempt on 8 November, when a bomb went off in a Munich beer cellar where he had been addressing supporters. Hitler left the building shortly before the explosion, which killed seven people and injured 63 more.

Krafft himself immediately broadcast news of his successful prediction by telegraphing Rudolf Hess. Hitler and his propaganda chief Joseph Goebbels were quickly informed, and Krafft was taken into custody by the Gestapo as a possible accomplice in the blast. He managed to convince them of his innocence, and eventually received the reward he had hoped for: Goebbels decided to give him a job.

Prediction and propaganda

The work that Krafft was set to do was not at all what he had expected. A passionate believer in astrology, he had hoped to cast horoscopes and advise politicians and generals on their future course of action. But Goebbels had other ideas. Shortly before Krafft had come to his attention, Goebbels' wife had shown him a quatrain by Nostradamus (see pages 116–121). It read: "Seven times you will see the British nation change/Steeped in blood for 290 years/Not at all free as a result of German support /Aries [God of War] fears his Bastarnian Pole." The Bastarni were a tribe that inhabited Poland in classical times, and the verse was interpreted to mean that, after six changes of British government or dynasty over a period of 290 years, a seventh would occur as a result of a situation involving Germany and Poland. If the first change after Nostradamus's time was taken to be the execution of Charles I and the establishment of the Commonwealth in 1649, the 290-year period expired in 1939.

Goebbels, in the event, was less interested in the Nostradamus prophecy itself than in the propaganda value of such messages, and he set Krafft to devising fake quatrains that could assist the Nazi war effort. The first results of Krafft's efforts were leaflets dropped on France at the time of the German invasion in 1940. These purported to show that Germany would conquer much of the country but leave the southeast unoccupied; the plan was to clog the roads with refugees headed in that direction, thereby hindering French troop movements.

While Krafft laboured on propaganda, another horoscope – one of which he had no knowledge – was to have a dramatic influence on his own life as well as on the course of the war. This was an anonymous reading,

> "There is a possibility of an assassination attempt using explosive material."
>
> (KARL ERNST KRAFFT PREDICTING THE 1939 MUNICH BOMB PLOT AGAINST HITLER A WEEK BEFORE THE EVENT)

reportedly drawn up in November 1918, on the future prospects for the German nation. No copy has survived, but the chart apparently foresaw Germany's fortunes in the ascendant up to May 1941, after which they would go into decline. This prediction was known to Rudolf Hess and seemingly weighed heavily on his mind, the more so as he knew that German forces would be invading Russia the following month, opening up the disturbing prospect of a war on two fronts. Hess's fears inspired his famous flight to Britain in May 1941 to try to arrange peace between the two nations. The mission was, of course, abortive, and Hess remained in prison for the next 46 years until his death in 1987.

The results of Hess's defection proved disastrous for Krafft and his fellow astrologers. Hitler ordered a clampdown on the "fortune-tellers and other swindlers", whom he blamed for Hess's actions. Krafft found himself in prison along with many other practitioners of the art. He was released in 1943 and set back to propaganda work, but the integrity of his forecasts soon told against him. Earlier in the war, for example, he had compared the horoscopes of Rommel and Montgomery, rival commanders in North Africa, and concluded that Montgomery's was definitely the stronger. Such frankness, and Krafft's bitter complaints at the demeaning work he was expected to do, led to his rearrest in 1944. He was held in poor conditions, caught typhus fever, and eventually died en route to the Buchenwald concentration camp in 1945. Sometime before his death, he made a final prediction: British bombs, he said, would fall on the propaganda ministry where he had been so shabbily treated. They duly did.

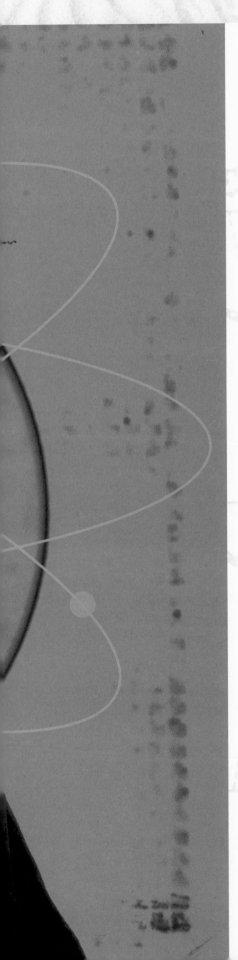

thinking the future

The twentieth century saw science take over from religion as the principal source of prophecy. The trend had been germinating for a long time – its origins can be traced all the way back to the Renaissance and to the work of such individuals as Leonardo da Vinci and Sir Thomas More. Where earlier prophets drew their inspiration from the gods, modern seers have increasingly sought to predict coming events by human reason alone. By a controlled effort of the imagination, they have tried to *think* the future – both how it is likely to develop and, in the case of More's seminal *Utopia* and its successors, how they would wish it to be.

Over the past half-century, prediction has even become big business. Hundreds of thousands of individuals around the world now earn their living through forecasting everything from economic and demographic trends to the likelihood of earthquakes or tomorrow's weather. In a few limited fields the forecasters have made great strides, but elsewhere the track record is at best chequered. As the third millennium dawns, the future remains, for the most part, as unpredictable as ever.

Leonardo, the Renaissance visionary

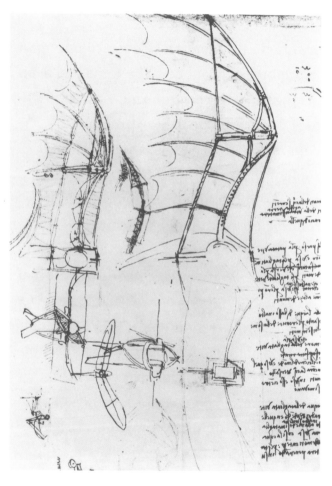

Born in 1452 in the Italian town of Vinci from which he was to take his name, Leonardo has come to be seen as the very model of a Renaissance man. Revered today as the painter responsible for the *Mona Lisa* and other masterpieces, he was above all a man of unquenchable intellectual curiosity, driven by a compulsive desire to understand how nature (and machinery) worked. Among the subjects to which he put his mind in the course of his

Leonardo's design for the "ornihopter" flying machine. The wings were intended to be flapped by a man using his arms and legs via a system of tackle lines and joints. Although the machine was too heavy to fly, the arch of the wings indicate that Leonardo correctly recognized the principles of aerodynamics.

astonishing 50-year career were not just art and aesthetics but also mathematics, astronomy, botany, and animal and human anatomy, of which he made important pioneering studies.

At first sight, the practical bent of Leonardo's genius might seem to lie at the opposite end of the spectrum of human potential from the prophetic spirit. Yet the scope of his curiosity was sufficiently wide to carry him well beyond the normal bounds of invention into territory normally associated more with visionaries and seers than with scientists or engineers. His prophetic gift expressed itself in what he called "pre-imagining" – the visualizing of the way things might be at some future time. The startling accuracy of some of his forecasts can in fact be traced back to his clear grasp of basic scientific principles and his intuitive skill in applying them in ways that the rest of the world would not catch up with for centuries to come.

The evidence of Leonardo's foresight is found in his notebooks, some 5,000 pages of which have survived. There, in a confused jumble of words and images, he sketched out invention after invention: a mechanical excavator; a machine for grinding mirrors; a rolling mill; an instrument for measuring wind speeds. All were noted down only for his own enlightenment in a curious mirror writing, written backwards with his left hand.

This parachute was built to one of Leonardo's designs using only tools and materials that would have been available in the 15th century. In 2000 a skydiver used it successfully to make a 7000-foot (2,100-m) descent from a hot-air balloon.

Foreseeing human flight

One of Leonardo's most passionate concerns was with the principles of flight. In his notebooks he not only meticulously copied the structure of birds' and bats' wings but also gave detailed instructions for making artificial models using wood, taffeta and fustian. Casually, in the corner of a page, he sketched a prototype parachute, writing beside it, "If a man have a tent made of linen of which the apertures have all been stopped up ..., he will be able to throw himself down from any great height without sustaining injury". This vision was to be realized more than 500 years later, when a British skydiver finally proved that the parachute Leonardo had sketched would indeed function correctly (see photograph, above).

Leonardo also sketched imaginary flying machines and helicopter-like mechanisms (see illustration, opposite). There are hints, too, that his interest in this subject went beyond simple intellectual curiosity; at one time he seems to have nurtured a serious ambition to master the power of flight. Again the clues are in the notebooks, in the form of cryptic messages: "The great bird will take its first flight from the back of the great swan, dumb-founding the universe, overwhelming with its renown all writings, and bringing eternal glory to its birthplace"; or "From the mountain bearing the name of the great bird, the famous bird will take flight that shall fill the world with its great renown." The two statements make more sense in the light of the fact that a high hill near Florence was known at the time as Monte Ceceri, or Mount Swan. Yet if Leonardo was indeed prophesying that he would be the first birdman, his prediction remained unfulfilled — the restless genius soon dropped his aeronautical studies to move on to fresh fields of discovery.

Apocalyptic predictions

Late in life Leonardo — frustrated at not having achieved all he felt himself capable of, and increasingly disillusioned with humankind's destructive nature — revealed a more traditional visionary strand in his nature. Like an Old Testament prophet, he took to imagining apocalyptic disasters that might one day sweep away all creation. In his notebooks he depicted the scene in the form of a cataclysmic deluge reminiscent of the biblical Flood. The great artist brought a meticulous eye for detail to the minutiae of the cataclysm, describing the collapsing hillsides that further forced up the water level and the debris of "tables, beds, boats and other improvised craft", each with its complement of terrified people and animals, floating over the submerged fields. Leonardo's vision of the Apocalypse shared the unique combination of qualities that characterized all his work: precise in all its parts, yet with an epic grandeur in its scope and scale.

utopia and its neighbours

Historically, one of the main forms of rational speculation about the future has been through so-called utopian fiction, depicting imaginary societies distant in time or place from the author's own. The genre takes its name from Thomas More's *Utopia*, published in 1516; the title is a double pun, playing on the Greek *outopos*, "nowhere", but also on *eutopos*, "a good place". However, even when More was writing, he was aware of earlier examples from classical times – he himself cites Plato's *Republic*.

The writers who described utopias – for there were many more of them in the wake of More – were generally interested in the existing state of society and how it could be bettered. Until the birth of science fiction in quite

Over the centuries, many artists, as well as writers, have been influenced by utopian ideals. The French painter Paul Signac created Au temps de l'harmonie – L'age d'or n'est pas dans le passé, il est dans l'avenir *("In the era of harmony – The golden age is not in the past, it is in the future") in 1893 or 1895.*

recent times, writers did not specifically set out to predict what the future might bring. Yet by speculating on how their own societies could be improved, they inevitably created blueprints for social development. Some became prophets by default, as their writings helped to bring about, at least in part, the world they had described.

More was a young man when he wrote *Utopia*. A brilliant barrister and a friend of the great Renaissance humanist Desiderius Erasmus, he was on the threshold of a career that would see him rise, 13 years later, to the highest post in the land, that of Lord Chancellor of England. More was also a man of principle whose beliefs eventually brought him into conflict with his master, King Henry VIII. When Henry decided to break with Rome and set up an independent Church of England, More refused to accept the change, and was beheaded for treason on London's Tower Hill in 1535.

More's main aim in writing *Utopia* was conservative. He mourned the passing of an older England, symbolized by the communal village system of the Middle Ages, and its replacement by a market economy, permitting "the rich man to buy up all". In the light of More's political instincts it is all the more surprising to find that, insofar as his social vision suggests anything in the modern world, it is Chairman Mao's China.

A precursor of Communism?

More's Utopia is an agricultural state in which property is held in common and no private enterprise is allowed. The only distinctions between individuals are based on rank and merit, not class. Society is organized around farm units supporting at least 40 people, although in Utopia, unlike in Mao's China, these are family-oriented. The working day is limited to six hours, and there are early-morning lectures for those seeking self-improvement. Meals are taken in public to the accompaniment of edifying readings. There is even a regular interchange of workers from the cities to the countryside and vice versa, to prevent the urban population from losing its roots in the soil.

Riches and ostentation of all sorts are despised. In Utopia, chamber pots are made of gold and silver to bring precious metals into disrepute, and jewels are viewed as children's playthings; when one foreign ambassador arrives bedecked in jewelry, he is greeted derisively for looking "as if he was still a little child". Clothing is simple in style and made for hard wear, not show. Gambling is forbidden, and there is also a prohibition on lawyers, "so there shall be less circumstance of words, and the truth sooner come to light". Courting couples are encouraged to see each other naked before marriage, in order to avoid sexual incompatibility, but sexual relations outside marriage are fiercely condemned, the culpable being punished by "most grievous bondage".

In other respects, however, Utopia remains markedly un-Maoist. Religion is central to its life, though its faith is of a reasonable and unoppressive kind – its priests are "of exceeding holiness, and therefore very few". There is a general emphasis on compassion and kindness. Hunting animals is condemned as "the lowest, vilest and most abject form of butchery"; and butchery itself – the slaughter of cattle – is considered so corrupting that it is

Gulliver and the moons of Mars

One of the great chance hits of prediction came in Jonathan Swift's classic imaginary-worlds novel, *Gulliver's Travels*, which was published in 1726. In describing the advanced sciences of the floating island of Laputa (see illustration, page 141), Swift mentioned that Laputan astronomers had discovered "two lesser stars, or satellites, which revolve about Mars". This was more than 150 years before the two moons of Mars, Phobos and Deimos, were first observed by Asaph Hall, working at the US Naval Observatory in Washington DC in 1877. Swift further specified that the two moons orbited the planet at distances equivalent to respectively three and five times the planet's diameter, and that the duration of their orbits was 10 and 21.5 hours. The actual distances are approximately 1.5 and 3.5 times the planet's diameter, and the sidereal periods 8 and 30 hours.

left to a small class of bondsmen who are denied full citizenship. To the Utopian mind, war is hateful and inglorious; when the possibility arises, it is thought better to assassinate an enemy leader than to see thousands of soldiers die. If warfare turns out to be inevitable, the Utopians prefer to use mercenaries in combat – they themselves only fight as a last resort.

In very modern vein, More uses framing devices to distance himself from his own narrative. He presents it as a tale picked up on an actual trip he made to the Low Countries in 1515 from a Portuguese mariner who had sailed with Amerigo Vespucci (the real-life explorer who gave his name to America). More even uses distancing to comment objectively on his own creation – he presents Utopia as an interesting alternative society, attractive in some respects, impractical in others. His work proved an immediate success. The book was translated into most major European languages (including English, for More wrote in Latin), and it spawned a host of imitations.

Salomon's House
One of the most interesting works inspired by *Utopia* was Francis Bacon's unfinished *New Atlantis*, written in 1626.

> "The end of our foundation is the knowledge of causes, and secret motions of things, and the enlarging of the bounds of human empire, to the effecting of all things possible."
>
> (Francis Bacon describes the aim of the science academy foreseen in his *New Atlantis*, partly realized in the founding of the Royal Society in London 34 years later)

If More's work reflected Renaissance humanism, Bacon's was the product of the dawning age of science. It too takes as its setting a newly discovered island, this one called Bensalem and located somewhere in the Pacific. Much of the work is given over to the description of a single institution, a prototype scientific academy – known as Salomon's House or the College of the Six Days' Works – that plays a central role in the running of the state. There was good reason for the emphasis: Bacon, an ambitious man, had hopes of persuading his one-time patron King James I (who liked to be referred to as "the new Solomon") to establish just such an institution in England.

Bacon's seekers engage in co-operative research in fields as diverse as physics, chemistry, astronomy, agriculture and medicine. To ensure that their work has practical applications, the college employs three "benefactors", whose job is "to bend themselves, looking into the experiments of their fellows, and cast about how to draw out of them things of use and practice for men's life and knowledge". This concern for the appliance of science pays off in technological advances: Bensalemites can fly and travel underwater, and have developed a form of microphone. They also pursue some of modern science's less appealing paths, including vivisection and inter-species genetic experiments.

Bacon's work was to prove highly prophetic in one important respect: its central idea was subsequently realized, at least in part, in the foundation of the Royal Society in London in 1660. Like Salomon's House, the society is devoted to encouraging interdisciplinary scientific co-operation. However, as Bacon's ideas were very much in the minds of the people who lobbied for the creation of the society, this should probably be classed at least in part as a self-fulfilling prediction.

Totalitarianism foreseen
The Italian Tommaso Campanella, a contemporary of Bacon's, was also fascinated by the possibilities of science. In Campanella's case, the enthusiasm was to prove dangerous – he was a Dominican monk, and his interest in the new ideas brought him into conflict with the Church. His radical politics also got him into trouble,

An illustration of the floating island of Laputa, home to a scientifically advanced society, from a 1910 edition of the 18th-century novel Gulliver's Travels *by Jonathan Swift. In outlining the knowledge of the Laputan astronomers, Swift described the two moons of Mars with remarkable accuracy (see box, page 139).*

month and changed four times a year. Sex is rigorously policed, and is "not for the pleasure of the individual but for the good of the republic". The magistrates decide who should sleep with whom on the basis of eugenic considerations. For example, fat men are mated with thin women and vice versa in order to produce satisfactorily proportioned children. Astrologers and doctors in consultation determine a propitious hour for the coupling, and at the due time, "when digestion is complete and they have prayed", the lucky pair are ushered into a bedroom decorated with "handsome statues of illustrious men, so that the women, seeing them, can ask the Lord to give them attractive children".

One of Campanella's more original ideas was to decorate the walls of his city with instructional artwork, illustrating everything from mathematical formulae to the different forms of animal and vegetable life, along with accompanying explanatory captions. Optimistically, he believed that children exposed to this ubiquitous pedagogic advertising would complete their education by the age of 10. Thereafter they could look forward to a life of unremitting labour since, for male citizens at least, "the most tiring work is considered the most praiseworthy".

However well-intentioned, the City of the Sun is incontestably totalitarian, and it was the fate of utopias generally to lose much of their appeal as the prospect of actual totalitarianism became a reality. As societies became more organized and controlled, the prospect of authoritarian rulers dictating every aspect of a citizen's life, even with the best of motives, came to seem less and less attractive. By the twentieth century the process was complete – Utopia, where all was for the best, gave way to Dystopia, a nightmare land of subjection and despair. The route from More's imaginary island, it turned out, led not to the ideal society but rather to Huxley's *Brave New World* and Orwell's *Nineteen Eighty-Four*.

with the result that he wrote his best-known work, *The City of the Sun*, in the course of a 27-year stretch in the prisons of the Inquisition.

In the light of Campanella's personal tribulations, it comes as rather a disappointment to find that his ideal city is a deeply unattractive place. Built on a hill somewhere in the East, the City of the Sun is run on almost monastic lines by an austere philosopher-ruler, the Metaphysician, who is chosen for his encyclopedic knowledge. He is supported by three chief aides whose titles are respectively Power, Wisdom and Love.

These individuals exert almost total control over the lives of the citizens, who at their behest have to move house every six months so as not to develop any dangerous attachment to personal property. Everyone wears identical white, ankle-length robes, washed once a

Jules verne and the technological imagination

Born in 1828, Jules Verne was was one of nineteenth-century France's best-selling authors. His novels, which poured out at the rate of one or two a year, won him great fame and fortune, enabling him to indulge in such luxuries as buying what was at the time the world's biggest yacht. Yet Verne's life was quite reclusive – the great inventor of fantastic voyages himself rarely travelled, and the pioneer delineator of air travel made only a single balloon ascent, from the provincial city of

Amiens, where he lived for the last 33 years of his life until his death in 1905.

Verne's preferred mode of travel was the imagination. Although not himself a scientist, he was fascinated by the possibilities opened up by the scientific advances of his day. By projecting forward from the state of knowledge in his time, he was able to come up with remarkably far-sighted visions of what the future held in store. In doing so, he helped inspire genuine pioneers. Charles William Beebe, the American ocean explorer who reached a depth of 3,028 feet (923 m) in a bathysphere in 1934, was an admirer of Verne's 1870 novel *Twenty Thousand Leagues Under the Sea*. Admiral Richard Byrd, who claimed to have made the first flight over the North Pole in 1926, said, "It is Jules Verne who guides me here".

Predictions in fiction

The list of Verne's predictions is long, and some of them have yet to be realized. From the time of his first novel, *Five Weeks in a Balloon*, published in 1863, he was inspired by the potential of flight. At the centre of his novel *The Clipper of the Clouds*, published in 1886, are heavier-than-air machines – its hero not only successfully builds one, but also subsequently devises another machine that can travel with equal ease on air, land and water. The *Nautilus* in *Twenty Thousand Leagues Under the Sea* is an ocean-going submarine imagined decades before the technology existed to make such vessels a reality – and a century before the first nuclear-powered submarines.

André Galland's cover for Twenty Thousand Leagues Under the Sea. *The submarine Jules Verne described in his novel was more ecologically friendly than its real-life successors: powered by electricity, its batteries were recharged from seawater, making it largely self-sufficient.*

> "we will reach the Moon, we will reach the planets, we will reach the stars with the same ease, speed and security with which we now travel from Liverpool to New York."
>
> (JULES VERNE PREDICTING SPACE TRAVEL IN HIS 1865 NOVEL *FROM THE EARTH TO THE MOON*)

Many of Verne's imaginings presage more recent innovations. In one novel, members of a town council communicate with one another from home by a system suggestive of both the telex and e-mail. He foresaw elevators and moving walkways, and described air-conditioned skyscrapers 980 feet (300 m) high, in which the "temperature was always equable". Verne also prefigured subsequent technology-driven plot devices; in his novel *The Brothers Kip* (1902), a murder is solved by massively enlarging a detail of a photograph, just as one was revealed 65 years later in Michelangelo Antonioni's celebrated film *Blow-Up*.

Verne's most remarkable predictive success came, however, with his third novel, *From the Earth to the Moon* (1865), and its successor *Round the Moon*, published five years later. Many authors before Verne had speculated about a lunar journey, but his account came much closer to the realities of the 1969 *Apollo 11* flight (see page 120) than anything his predecessors had managed. Some of the coincidences between the two are startling. Verne's imagined moonshot started from Tampa, Florida, less than 125 miles (200 km) from Cape Kennedy, where the *Apollo* lift-off occurred. Verne correctly visualized rockets being used to shift the craft in and out of lunar orbit – this almost four decades before the Wright brothers had made the first powered flight – and had the spacecraft splashing down in the Pacific Ocean on its return to Earth. Most amazing of all was Verne's reckoning of the time the journey would take. His travellers reached the Moon in 97 hours and 13 minutes, where the *Apollo 11* astronauts took 97 hours and 39 minutes.

Yet for all the similarities, Verne's imagination was bounded by the technological limitations of his time. His spacecraft was a projectile, fired from the barrel of a 900-foot (275-m) long gun. Even more bizarrely to modern eyes, his astronauts travelled in smoking jackets and took along two dogs for company.

Toward the end of his life, Verne became more concerned with the misuse of technology. In novels such as *Propeller Island* (1895) and the posthumously published *The Barsac Mission*, he envisaged totalitarian worlds in which technology was used not to free people but to enslave them. Horrors such as fragmentation bombs, remote-control drones and electric torture instruments dotted their pages – and, sadly, Verne turned out to be just as prescient in his pessimism as he had been in his youthful, idealistic dreams of liberation through technology.

America in the year 2889

One of Verne's less-known works, written for a US magazine in 1889, made playful predictions as to what life might be like in America one thousand years later. Writing at a time when the European powers still dominated the globe, Verne already visualized the USA as a superpower – one that had not merely annexed the entire American continent but that now had England as a colony. Within his future America, media magnates ruled supreme, masters of an empire of "telephonic journalism" – his prevision of broadcasting. He also predicted a webcam-like device called a "phonotelephote" that allowed people thousands of miles apart to see and talk to one another. The environmental news, though, was mostly bad: Verne foresaw a land in which huge advertisements were beamed up to the sky, and the entire countryside was crisscrossed by electrical cables like a giant spider's web.

The prophet of the modern age

Of all the technology prophets of the early modern world, none has stood the test of time as well as H.G. Wells. There were, of course, many things that Wells missed and much that he got wrong. But the picture of modern life that he painted 100 years ago is still recognizable today, and in some of the details included in his novels, his writing was eerily prescient.

Wells's success is the more extraordinary in the light of his background. Born into a poor family in 1866, he was taken out of school at the age of 14 to work as a draper's assistant. Through his own efforts, he subsequently won a scholarship to study in London at the Normal School for Science, and in his 20s he finally found his vocation as a popular novelist and journalist. He went on to write more than 100 books and numerous articles, achieving considerable fame in his own lifetime. It was the combination of technological curiosity, stimulated by his scientific studies, and the sociological concerns encouraged by his journalistic bent that allowed Wells to visualize not just how the machine age might develop, but also what its social effects might be.

The fruit of his speculations appeared in a work called *Anticipations*, published in 1901. At a time when the first cars were appearing on the roads, Wells set out to imagine what shape a future motor age might take. He visualized road-haulage firms and long-distance buses, and waxed lyrical on the freedom to travel at will that private motor cars would bring. He foresaw freeways and even flyovers, noting that "where their ways branch, the streams of traffic will not cross at a level, but by bridges". He was equally clear-sighted about the likely social effects of cars, foreseeing the growth of long-distance commuting. He noted that, "It is not too much to say that the London citizen of the year 2000 AD may have a choice of nearly all England

An illustration of a scene from H.G. Wells's The War of the Worlds, *showing the Martians, who have invaded Earth, attacking a battleship. Published in 1898, the novel foresaw the development and use of gas warfare, laser-like weapons and industrial robots. Its description of gigantic guns launching space vehicles may have been inspired by Jules Verne's* From the Earth to the Moon *(see page 143).*

and Wales south of Nottingham and east of Exeter as his suburb". Wells also predicted that New York's workers of the future would be able to live in a commuter hinterland stretching from Albany to Washington DC.

Socially, Wells foresaw the expansion of the middle classes and of the educational system to meet the needs of an increasingly skilled and literate populace. He imagined the houses in which the new citizens would live, where there would be no servants as in his own day – instead, housework would be minimized by science. He imagined a kind of air conditioning: " ... air will enter the house of the future through proper tubes in the walls, which will warm it and capture its dust, and it will be spun out again by a simple mechanism." Cookery in 1900 still meant open ranges and cooks slaving over hot plates "with a crimsoned face and bare, blackened arms". But this would change, Wells wrote, for "with a neat little range, heated by electricity and provided with thermometers, with absolutely controllable temperatures and proper heat screens, cooking might very easily be made a pleasant amusement".

The pessimistic prophet

Yet Wells was far from being an unguarded optimist about the future. He also foresaw with startling clarity the future direction of warfare. Writing a dozen years before they were invented, he predicted the use of "land ironclads" – tanks – and the development of the modern rifle: " ... one can conceive it provided in the future with cross-thread telescopic sights, the focussing of which, corrected by some ingenious use of hygroscopic material, might even find the range." In his novel *The War in the Air* – published in 1908, barely four years after the Wright brothers' first flight – Wells presented the saturation bombing of cities as a threat to civilization. Most startlingly of all, he predicted the building of atomic bombs as early as 1914, even before the atom had been split, inventing an imaginary radioactive element called "carolinum" to do the job that uranium and plutonium were eventually to fulfill.

However, for all his far-sightedness and his huge success as a novelist, Wells died in 1946 an unhappy and very frustrated man. Throughout his life he had advocated solutions to the problems confronting humanity that included the abandonment of nationalism in favour of international government – for example, he was an early advocate of the League of Nations – and the need for education to prevent people from stumbling blindly into war. "Human life," he wrote, "becomes more and more a race between education and catastrophe." Yet, instead of the enlightenment he had hoped for, Wells lived to see the West plunging into the vortex of Fascism, Nazism and the terrible mass slaughter of the Second World War. In one of his last books, *Mind at the End of its Tether*, Wells wrote pessimistically, "The end of everything we call life is close at hand and cannot be evaded". In his final disillusionment, the apostle of progress ended up echoing the doomsday prophet's centuries-old cry of despair.

> "certainly it seems now that nothing could have been more obvious to the people of the early twentieth century than the rapidity with which war was becoming impossible. and as certainly they did not see it. they did not see it until the atomic bombs burst in their fumbling hands."
>
> (H.G. WELLS PREDICTING ATOMIC WARFARE AND ITS CONSEQUENCES IN HIS 1914 NOVEL *THE WORLD SET FREE*, FIVE YEARS BEFORE ERNEST RUTHERFORD FIRST SPLIT THE ATOM)

prediction as science

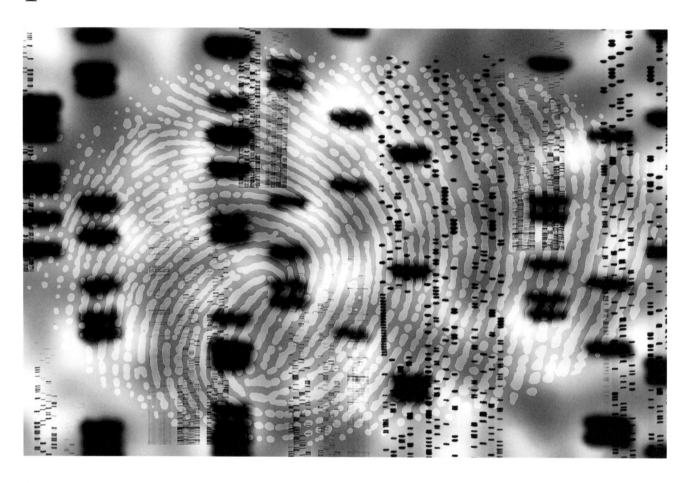

At the start of the third millennium, the market for prediction is bigger than it has ever been. No society has ever been more concerned with the future than our own, almost equally in hope of dazzling progress and in fear of ecological or nuclear disaster.

People in pursuit of knowledge of the future tend to take one of two markedly different paths. On the one hand, the appetite for fortune-telling of all kinds has continued to expand. Most Western cities support a small army of astrologers, tarot-card readers and crystal-ball gazers, while mass-media newspapers and magazines around the globe count horoscope columns among their most popular features. However, alongside this ancient tradition, which continues centuries-old methods of

A computer image of an autoradiogram of DNA sequences super-imposed over a human fingerprint — both are unique to each individual. Our rapidly growing understanding of genetics is opening up a range of new predictive possibilities. For example, DNA testing now allows geneticists to foresee whether or not a person is predisposed to develop certain inherited diseases in the future.

prediction in new packaging, a multi-billion dollar industry has grown up based purportedly on more scientific forms of prognostication.

The new experts work in many fields. There are physical scientists who forecast the likelihood of earth-quakes or volcanic eruptions or meteor or comet strikes. Demographers and actuaries study future population trends and the age at which growing generations are likely to fall ill and die. Whole battalions of management consultants and business strategists earn a living by advising companies and corporations on adapting their working methods to a changing world. Above all, an entire industry has grown up around economic forecasting, ranging from the specialists at the World Bank and the OECD, who seek to predict global patterns of wealth creation and distribution, to investment analysts focused on outguessing the stock market's next move.

One science that already offers genuine predictive possibilities is genetics. Its most obvious application lies in using knowledge of an individual's predisposition to illness to prevent the passing on of hereditary conditions. As an example of what can be achieved, the Committee for the Prevention of Jewish Genetic Diseases in the USA now organizes the testing of schoolchildren's blood. When a marriage is being considered, a matchmaker can telephone the organization and – using numbers assigned during testing rather than names, to ensure anonymity – can check whether the potential partners carry mutations responsible for either cystic fibrosis or the rare but lethal condition known as Tay-Sachs disease. If both do, the Committee advises against the match. The results have already been dramatic; cystic fibrosis in particular has been largely eradicated from the Jewish community.

A composite artwork shows a communications satellite orbiting the Earth. Such satellites are used to relay telephonic data and television signals – in short, they make the much-vaunted "global village" a reality. The high speed at which information can now be sent around the world has greatly assisted predictive sciences.

"A mind which, at a given moment, had full knowledge of all the forces vitalizing nature, and of the position of all the beings of which nature is composed ... would be able to apply one and the same formula to the motions of the celestial bodies and the lightest atoms alike. Nothing would be uncertain for such a mind, and past and future would be immediately present."

(THE MARQUIS DE LAPLACE, EIGHTEENTH-CENTURY FRENCH ASTRONOMER AND MATHEMATICIAN, EXPRESSING THE HOPE OF MAKING THE FUTURE SCIENTIFICALLY PREDICTABLE)

A meteorologist holds a weather balloon called a "Jimsphere" after its inventor, Jim Scoggins. The balloon, which is used to supply pre-launch wind data for ground-based rocket launches, carries instruments for measuring temperature and humidity at an altitude of up to about 10 miles (16 km). Once released, the Jimsphere is tracked visually or by radar to assess wind velocity.

Prophets of nature

In some fields the scientists have stepped directly into the old-fashioned diviners' shoes. Weather forecasting is a case in point. The need to foresee the prospects for drought or flood is at least as old as agriculture, and from the earliest times people have turned to individuals claiming special knowledge to find out what might be in store. When not reliant on astrology for forecasting, as in ancient Babylon, people turned instead to traditional weather-lore, a generally more accurate guide often based on close observation of nature. For example, certain plants were known to close their petals in advance of rain, and cattle huddled before a storm.

Change came slowly with the dawning of the scientific era. A major practical advance was made, first with the invention of the thermometer by the great Galileo and then, in 1644, of the barometer by Evangelista Torricelli. The barometer indicated coming weather prospects

by the movement of mercury in a tube. No serious theoretical progress was possible, however, until the concept of the Earth's atmosphere, where weather is formulated, finally emerged in the latter part of the seventeenth century.

Scientists collected increasing amounts of data on weather conditions in the eighteenth and early nineteenth centuries, but an effective international forecasting service had to wait on the development of the electric telegraph, which first permitted news of the weather to travel faster than the weather systems themselves. The first effective international forecasting network started operating out of Paris in 1860. Thereafter there was steady progress in refining the quality of forecasting, particularly in the early twentieth century in response to the growth of aviation, which provided a new and pressing market for up-to-the-minute information.

Today, weather forecasting is very big business indeed. In 1995 the World Meteorological Organization estimated that the global budget devoted to it was in the region of $4 billion US, about half of it in the USA alone. Meteorology is one of the relatively few fields in which forecasts are checked statistically for accuracy. The figures show that short-term forecasts (up to a couple of days ahead) are generally reliable, at least in predicting the big picture. However, long-range forecasts still rely essentially on the forward projection of past weather patterns, and are therefore intrinsically unreliable.

Even so, weather forecasting is one of the success stories of predictive science. Seismologists, for example, have made huge advances in understanding the Earth's subterranean movements, but experts are still a long way away from being able to predict earthquakes with anything like 100 per cent certainty.

Astronomers investigating large heavenly bodies work with a much greater degree of certainty about the future. The regular pattern underlying the Earth's recurrent close encounters with Halley's comet were first noted by Edmond Halley as long ago as 1704. However, smaller asteroids can still take observers by surprise. NASA is currently busy cataloguing asteroids with near-earth orbits, in the hope of listing 90 per cent of bodies more than 0.6 miles (1 km) in diameter by the year 2008.

Human sciences

When it comes to the human sciences, degrees of error in forecasting grow exponentially. Even estimating how many people will be alive at a given date – a basic calculation on which everything from future world food requirements to the level of individuals' pensions depends – is fraught with uncertainty. Over the past 50 years, demographers have been good at painting the big picture; predictions of the rise in the total world population have been largely realized. They have also been close to the mark in predicting increasing life expectancy in developed countries. But these successes have both involved the forward projection of a steady trend. Whenever there has been a break in the pattern – for instance, with the baby boom in the years after the Second World War – demographic calculations have invariably failed to spot the discontinuity and have been thrown out of kilter as a result.

Demographers, then, are skillful extrapolators, but they are not prophets. The same point applies with even greater force to economists. Economic forecasting has long been a growth area – by 1996, there were nearly 150,000 economists in the USA alone, most of them working in one way or another on forward projections. Huge sums of money are spent each year both by governments and businesses to predict coming economic trends. Yet results suggest that the outlay reflects the importance accorded to the subject rather than the reliability of the answers supplied. Economists have significantly failed to call the start or the end of any of the major post-war recessions. Investment specialists

have, by and large, proved no more far-sighted. It was the realization that, over time, even star fund managers failed significantly to beat the market that led to the rise in popularity of tracker funds in the 1990s.

The message, then, is fairly plain. Predictive science can be extraordinarily good at detecting past or present patterns or trends and extending these hypothetically into the future. It is, though, largely useless at foreseeing sudden breaks or accidents – precisely those cataclysmic changes that have traditionally been the field of inspired prophecy. The fact that "scientific forecasts" have taken on something of the prophet's mantle says more about the current prestige of science than its prophetic abilities. Maybe it is unreasonable to expect otherwise; when even the CIA, the US military and defence experts worldwide failed to predict in advance something as epoch-making as the collapse of the USSR and eastern-bloc Communism in the late 1980s, the limited capacity of expert knowledge to presage future events stands painfully exposed.

The millennium bug scare

The millennium bug scare in the months leading up to the year 2000 provided an object lesson in the limits of predictive science. News media around the world suggested at the time that widespread chaos would ensue because software embedded in computer systems, programmed to recognize only double-digit year endings, would mistake 2000 for 1900 and would effectively cease to function. Huge sums were spent on addressing the problem – the USA alone had a budget of $7.5 billion. Yet when 1 January 2001 dawned, none of the predicted disruption happened. Arguments that effective advance preparation had solved the problem were rendered unconvincing by the fact that even countries that had taken few precautions, such as Russia, emerged largely unscathed. The upshot showed that the media frenzy of late 1999 had turned a relatively minor technical problem into a classic, but inaccurate, pre-millennial prophecy of doom.

The Rise of Futurology

As growing numbers of people turned to science to learn about the future, it was perhaps inevitable that prediction itself should eventually spawn a science of its own. The word "futurology" was coined in the 1940s by a German political scientist, Ossip Flechtheim, building on the work of H.G. Wells (see pages 144–5) and others in outlining coming trends. In the post-war years, the new discipline rapidly became big business as research-and-development institutes and policy forums multiplied.

The Rand Corporation, which was set up in 1948 with funding from the US Air Force, was the prototype of the think tanks. Its best-known alumnus was Herman Kahn, a California Institute of Technology graduate researcher whom the corporation hired to work on questions of military strategy. Kahn's books on the subject, including *Thinking About the Unthinkable* (1962), made him a celebrity, and in 1961 he set up his own organization, the Hudson Institute. Other countries soon followed the American example, and today think tanks have proliferated around the world.

Other institutions devoted to speculation on the future have also flourished. The World Future Society, set up in 1966 and based in Washington DC, currently has 30,000 members internationally. Its board includes such well-known pundits as Arthur C. Clarke of *2001: A Space Odyssey* fame, Alvin Toffler, author of *Future Shock* and *The Third Wave*, and John Naisbitt, whose works include *Megatrends 2000*.

Dramatic advances in space technology have altered our perceptions of the universe. This image of a column of interstellar hydrogen gas in the Eagle Nebula 7,000 light-years from Earth was taken by the Hubble Space Telescope in 1995.

The futurology movement has had a profound impact on public attitudes and policy over the past 50 years, and a survey of its various successes and failures is beyond the scope of this book. However, what is interesting about futurology is that its development was itself entirely predictable.

Since the earliest times, the need for foreknowledge of the future has been most marked in periods of change and stress. The great biblical prophets (see pages 12–21) emerged not in the days of Israel's expansion, but when its people were at risk, divided between the kingdoms of Israel and Judah and threatened by the armies of Babylon or Assyria. The Native American seers (see pages 44–7) found their followings at a time when traditional ways of life were under threat and a tide of white settlement was sweeping across the continent. On a more personal level, history's traumatic moments – the sinking of the *Titanic* (see pages 66–7), major political assassinations, the 11 September 2002 assault on New York – tend to trigger a wave of individual predictive dreams and premonitions. Anxiety and uncertainty, it seems, create a demand for information that prophets then arise to answer.

Unsettling changes
The pace of technological and social change that has occurred since the end of the Second World War has been unparalleled in human history. Take world population growth. It took 100,000 years of human development for world population to top one billion, a point passed sometime early in the nineteenth century. By 1950 the total had risen to two and a half billion, and today it is well over six billion and rising. Associated with that phenomenon is increasing life expectancy, which rose gradually from the 20 or so years that Stone Age hunter-gatherers could have hoped for to 46.4 years by 1950. Since then the figure has risen exponentially, reaching a global average of 63 years by the year 2000, with the residents of developed countries generally able to expect 75 years.

The ever-increasing speed of technological development is equally unsettling. Commercial nuclear power, computers, transistors, space technology, lasers and fibre optics have swept the globe since the Second World War. The pace shows little sign of slowing down with the current growth of genetic research, nanotechnology and bioengineering.

In a landscape changing as fast as the scenery glimpsed from a speeding car's windscreen, people naturally tend to seek signposts. Futurologists help give a sense of direction by discerning patterns in the apparent chaos and pointing the way ahead. In doing so, they fulfil both of prophecy's traditional roles: like the old augurs and diviners they foretell what the future might have in store, and at the same time they inherit something of the inspired seers' task of telling individuals how to shape their lives to fit an evolving world.

In the past, when people looked to religion to explain the universe, prophecy wore a religious coat. Now that science has largely taken over that role, it is hardly surprising that people expect predictions to come in scientific clothing instead. Yet their hopes are, for the most part, likely to be disappointed. The future remains just as mysterious as ever. When it comes to foreseeing the big and unexpected changes that shape its course, sudden, unpredictable moments of insight are as likely to be right as the fastest and best-informed computer on Earth.

"The telephone may be appropriate for our American cousins but not here, because we have an adequate supply of messenger boys."

(THE CONCLUSION OF A BRITISH PANEL OF EXPERTS CONSIDERING THE FUTURE OF TELEPHONY IN THE LATE NINETEENTH CENTURY, AS QUOTED IN WILLIAM A. SHERDEN'S *THE FORTUNE SELLERS*)

further reading

Ashe, Geoffrey. *The Book of Prophecy*. Blandford: London, 1999.

Bacon, Francis. *The New Atlantis*. Kessinger: Mt. Kila, 1998).

Bander, Peter. *The Prophecies of St. Malachy*. Tan Books: Rockford, Ill., 1973.

Bascom, William. *Ifa Divination*. University of Indiana Press: Bloomington, 1969.

Besterman, Theodore. *Crystal-Gazing*. William Rider & Son: London, 1924.

Bloomfield, Paul. *Imaginary Worlds*. Hamish Hamilton: London, 1932.

Boyer, Paul. *When Time Shall Be No More*. Harvard University Press: Cambridge, Mass., 1992.

Campanella, Tommaso. *Oeuvres Choisies*. Lavigne: Paris, 1844.

Cheetham, Erika (ed.). *The Prophecies of Nostradamus*. Neville Spearman: London, 1973.

Chesneaux, Jean. *The Political and Social Ideas of Jules Verne*. Thames & Hudson: London, 1972.

Cohn, Norman. *The Pursuit of the Millennium*. Paladin: London, 1970.

Cottrell, John. *Anatomy of an Assassination*. Frederick Muller: London, 1966.

Davis, Andrew Jackson. *The Penetralia: Being Harmonial, Answers to Important Questions*. Bela Marsh: Boston, 1856.

Dee, Jonathan. *The Book of Prophecies*. Collins & Brown: London, 1999.

Douglas, Alfred. *The Tarot*. Victor Gollancz: London, 1972.

Dummett, Michael. *The Game of Tarot*. Duckworth: London, 1980.

Dummett, Michael, Decker, Ronald, and Depaulis, Thierry. *A Wicked Pack of Cards: The Origins of the Occult Tarot*. Duckworth: London, 1996.

Dunne, J.W. *An Experiment with Time*. Faber & Faber: London, 1958.

Durant, John. *Predictions*. A.S. Barnes & Co: New York, 1956.

Eliade, Mircea. *Shamanism*. Princeton University Press: New Jersey, 1972.

Fisher, Joe, with Commins, Peter. *Predictions*. Van Nostrand Reinhold: New York, 1980.

Gattey, Charles Neilson. *Prophecy and Prediction in the 20th Century*. Aquarian Press: Wellingborough, 1989.

Gattey, Charles Neilson. *They Saw Tomorrow*. Harrap: London, 1977.

Geoffrey of Monmouth. *The History of the Kings of Britain*. Penguin Books: Harmondsworth, 1966.

Gibson, Walter B. and Litzka, R. *The Encyclopaedia of Prophecy*. Granada: London, 1977.

Glass, Justine. *The Story of Fulfilled Prophecy*. Cassell: London, 1969.

Gould, Lt.-Comm. Rupert T. *Oddities: A Book of Unexplained Facts*. Geoffrey Bles: London, 1944

Graves, Robert. *The Greek Myths*. Folio Society: London, 1996.

Hammond, J.R. *An H.G.Wells Companion*. Macmillan: London, 1979.

Hemming, John. *The Conquest of the Incas*. Macmillan: London, 1970.

Hillegas, Mark R. *The Future as Nightmare*. Oxford University Press: New York, 1967.

Hopkins, James K. *A Woman to Deliver Her People: Joanna Southcott and English Millenarianism in an Era of Revolution*. University of Texas Press: Austin, 1982.

Hort, G.M. *Dr. John Dee: Elizabethan Mystic and Astrologer*. William Rider & Son: London, 1922.

Kahn, Herman, Brown, William, and Martel, Leon. *The Next 200 Years: A Scenario for America in the World*. William Morrow: New York, 1976.

Leach, Maria, and Fried, Jerome (ed.). *Funk &Wagnall's Standard Dictionary of Folklore, Mythology, and Legend*. HarperCollins: San Francisco, 1984.

Lewinsohn, Richard. *Prophets and Prediction: A History of Prophecy from Babylon to Wall Street*. Secker & Warburg: London, 1961.

Loewe, Michael, and Blacker, Carmen (ed.). *Divination and Oracles*. George Allen & Unwin: London, 1981.

Mackenzie, Alexander. *The Prophecies of the Brahan Seer*. Eneas Mackay: Stirling, 1899.

Maclean, Shirley. *Mother Shipton and her Prophecies*. Self-published, undated.

Macneice, Louis. *Astrology*. Bloomsbury: London, 1989.

Matthews, John (ed.). *The World Atlas of Divination*. BCA: London, 1992.

Miller, Mary, and Taube, Karl. *The Gods and Symbols of Ancient Mexico and the Maya*. Thames & Hudson: London, 1993.

More, Thomas. *Utopia*. Penguin Classics: Harmondsworth, 1965.

Parke, H.W., and Wormell, D.E.W. *The Delphic Oracle*. Blackwell: Oxford, 1956.

Parker, Derek and Julia. *A History of Astrology*. Andre Deutsch: London, 1983.

Reeves, Marjorie. *Joachim of Fiore and the Prophetic Future*. Harper & Row: New York, 1977.

Reeves, Marjorie. *The Influence of Prophecy in the Later Middle Ages*. University of Notre Dame Press: Notre Dame, Ind., 1993.

Ridley, Matt. *Genome*. Fourth Estate: London, 1999.

Robertson, Morgan. *The Wreck of the Titan, or Futility*. Amereon: New York, 1995.

Sherden, William A. *The Fortune Sellers*. John Wiley & Sons: New York, 1998.

Spence, Jonathan D. *God's Chinese Son*. W.W. Norton & Co: New York, 1996.

Stearn, Jess. *Edgar Cayce – The Sleeping Prophet*. Doubleday & Co: New York, 1963.

Sugden, John. *Tecumseh*. Henry Holt & Co: New York, 1998.

Thomas, Keith. *Religion and the Decline of Magic*. Weidenfeld & Nicolson: London, 1971.

Time-Life Books, (eds.). *Dreams and Dreaming*. Time-Life Books: Amsterdam, 1990.

Time-Life Books, (eds.). *Visions and Prophecies*. Time-Life Books: Amsterdam, 1988.

Tolstoy, Nikolai. *The Quest for Merlin*. Hamish Hamilton: London, 1985.

Verne, Jules. *20,000 Leagues Under the Sea*. Oxford University Press: New York, 1998.

Verne, Jules. *Five Weeks in a Balloon*. Pyramid: New York, 1962.

Verne, Jules. *From the Earth to the Moon*. Bantam Classics: New York, 1993.

Verne, Jules. *Propeller Island*. Panther: London, 1965.

Verne, Jules. *The Barsac Mission*. Amereon: New York, 1976.

Verne, Jules. *The Clipper of the Clouds*. Sampson Low, Marston & Co: London, 1920.

Von Dollinger, John J.I. *Prophecies and the Prophetic Spirit in the Christian Era*. Rivingstons: London, 1873.

Wagar, W. Warren (ed.). *H.G.Wells: Journalism and Prophecy 1893–1946*. Bodley Head: London, 1964.

Wallechinsky, David, and Wallace, Amy and Irving. *The Book of Predictions*. Corgi: London, 1982.

Wanley, Nathaniel. *The Wonders of the Little World*. London, 1788.

Weber, Eugen. *Apocalypses*. Hutchinson: London, 1999.

Wells, H.G. *Anticipations of the Reaction of Mechanical and Scientific Progress upon Human Life and Thought*. Chapman & Hall: London, 1902.

Wells, H.G. *The War in the Air*. G. Bell & Sons: London, 1908.

Wells, H.G. *The World Set Free*. Corgi: London, 1976.

West, Jr., Ray B. *Kingdom of the Saints*. Jonathan Cape: London, 1958.

Wilhelm, Richard (trans.). *The I Ching or Book of Changes*. Routledge & Kegan Paul: London, 1951.

index

References to captions are in *italics*.

picture credits

The publisher would like to thank the following people, museums, and photographic libraries for permission to reproduce their material. Every care has been taken to trace copyright holders. However, if we have omitted anyone we apologize, and will, if informed, make corrections in any future edition.

AA = Art Archive, London
BAL = Bridgeman Art Library, London
MEPL = Mary Evans Picture Library, London
SPL = Science Photo Library, London

2 AA/Musée des Beaux Arts, Besançon/Dagli Orti; 4 BAL/Warburg Institute; 6 AKG London; 7 BAL, London/Private Collection; 8–9 BAL/Tabley House, University of Manchester (John Martin: *The Destruction of Herculaneum and Pompeii*); 10 Corbis/Canadian Museum of Civilization; 11 Corbis/Tom Bean; 12 Scala, Florence/Palace of the Popes, Avignon; 15 BAL/Giraudon/Musée d'Unterlinden, Colmar; 16 AA/Museo del Prado, Madrid/Dagli Orti; 18 AA/Museo Correr, Venice/Dagli Orti; 19 AKG London/Galleria Nazionale dell'Umaria/S Domingie; 20 BAL/Detroit Institute of Arts; 22 BAL/Vatican Museums and Galleries; 24 BAL/Staatliche Museen, Berlin; 25 AKG London/Louvre, Paris; 27 Corbis/K M Westermann; 28 Corbis/Mimmo Jodice; 29 Scala, Florence/Duomo, Siena; 30 Corbis/Stephanie Colosanti; 31 Corbis/Gianni Dagli Orti; 32 Axiom Photographs, London/Chris Coe; 33 Corbis/National Gallery, London; 34 Scala, Florence/Biblioteca Statale, Lucca; 36 Corbis/Archivo Iconografico, S.A.; 37 Stone; 38 BAL/Private Collection; 39 BAL/Louvre, Paris; 40 Corbis/Royal Ontario Museum/Richard Swiecki; 41 AA/The School of Oriental and African Studies, London/Eileen Tweedy; 42 BAL/Yale University Art Gallery, New Haven, CT; 43 MEPL; 44 AKG London; 45 Corbis/Stapleton Collection; 47 BAL/Museum of the North American Indian, New York; 48 Fortean Picture Library; 49 Corbis/Bettmann; 50–51 Corbis/Bettman (the *Titanic*); 52 Michael Holford, London/Royal Dutch Cabinet of Medals, The Hague; 53 BAL/Louvre; 54 Corbis/Gianni Dagli Orti; 55 AKG London/Gilles Mermet; 56 Werner Forman Archive, London/Liverpool Museum; 58 BAL/Private Collection; 61 AA/Eileen Tweedy; 62 Corbis/Bettmann; 63 AKG, London/Musée Rolin, Autun/Joseph Martin; 65 Corbis/Hulton Getty; 66 Corbis/Bettmann; 67 AA/Ocean Memorabilia Collection; 68 AKG London; 70 Corbis; 72–73 AKG London/François Guenet (Tomb of Seti); 74 AKG London/Louvre, Paris/Erich Lessing; 75 Corbis/Charles & Josette Lenars; 76 AKG London/Musée Condé, Chantilly; 78 Corbis/Royal Ontario Museum/Richard Swiecki; 79 Robert Harding Picture Library, London/Occidor; 80 Michael Holford, London/Wellcome Collection, London; 82 AKG London/Justus Göpel; 83 BAL/Yale Center for British Art, Paul Mellon Collection, USA; 84 Scala, Florence; 85 Scala, Florence/Museo Civico, Piacenza; 87 AA/Galleria d'Arte Moderna, Rome/Dagli Orti (A); 88 BAL/Bibliothèque Nationale, Paris; 89 BAL, London/Private Collection; 90 AKG London/Louvre, Paris/Erich Lessing; 92 Hutchison Library, London/Mick Czaky; 93 Werner Forman Archive, London/Entwistle Gallery, London; 94 AA/National Museum of Anthropology, Mexico City/Dagli Orti; 95 AKG London/Evelyn Hean; 96 AKG London/Museo de America; 98 BAL/Ashmolean Museum, Oxford; 99 Werner Forman Archive, London/British Museum, London; 100 BAL/Private Collection; 102 MEPL; 103 MEPL; 104–105 BAL/Harris Museum and Art Gallery, Preston (William Shackleton: *City of the Golden Gates*); 106 BAL/ Lady Lever Art Gallery, Port Sunlight, Merseyside; 108 BAL/Lambeth Palace Library, London; 109 Mick Sharp, Caernarfon; 111 BAL/Sheffield Galleries and Museums Trust; 112 Bodleian Library, Oxford; 113 Fortean Picture Library, Ruthin, Wales/Janet & Colin Board; 114 MEPL; 115 BAL/British Library, London; 116 Corbis/Chris Hellier; 118 AA/University Library, Geneva/Dagli Orti; 119 AA/London Museum/Eileen Tweedy; 120 Hulton Archive, London/NASA; 122t BAL/National Gallery, London; 122b AA; 123 AA/Jean-Loup Charmet; 125 Corbis/Wild Country; 126 MEPL; 128 Corbis/Bettmann; 129 MEPL; 130 Corbis/Bettmann; 131 MEPL; 132 Hulton Getty, London; 134–135 SPL/James King-Holmes (grid of DNA fragments); 136 Science & Society Picture Library, London; 137 Gamma/Frank Spooner Pictures, London; 138 AKG London/Mairie de Montreuil, Paris/Erich Lessing; 141 AKG London; 142 BAL/Collection Kharbine-Tapabor, Paris. © ADAGP, Paris and DACS, London 2002; 144 SPL/David Hardy; 146 SPL/Alfred Pasieka; 147 SPL/David Ducros; 148 SPL/David Parker; 150 NASA/Hubble Space Telescope Image